praise for jacqueline mallorca and
GLUTEN-FREE ITALIAN

"The great thing about Jacqueline Mallorca's [...] icious dishes everyone can enjoy at anytime. There [...] cook separately for the gluten-sensitive guest. And [...] n sensitive, this book opens up the whole glory of Italian food."

—Gerald Asher, contributing editor, *Gourmet Magazine*

"Jackie Mallorca has done a masterful job of combining Italian cooking ideas and substitutes for Italian products celiacs are not to have. In this easy to understand and easy to make collection of recipes, celiacs have no worry about making a mistake. We who are not celiacs get to enjoy savory, tasty, traditional dishes that are very Italian in both concept and flavor."

—Darrell Corti, Corti Brothers Fine Wine and Gourmet Foods Italian Grocery Store

"From breakfast to dinner, the veteran food writer and Chronicle Food section contributor draws a delicious road map for people with celiac disease or other digestive problems that exclude gluten from the diet. In Mallorca's capable hands, rice, oat, and nut flours are turned into dishes that rival conventional wheat flour creations. Even pasta and desserts are not off limits."

—*San Francisco Chronicle* on *The Wheat-Free Cook*

"Mallorca offers inventive dishes such as chicken breasts with a hazelnut-Parmesan crust and five-minute trout with crispy caper sauce. She also includes an impressive selection of breakfasts, side dishes, and baked goods."

—*Associated Press* on *The Wheat-Free Cook*

"The true merit of *The Wheat-Free Cook* lies in its accessibility and broad appeal: One can learn how to be a more accommodating cook and how to put xanthan gum to good use."

—*Washington Post* on *The Wheat-Free Cook*

GLUTEN-FREE ITALIAN

ALSO BY JACQUELINE MALLORCA:

The Wheat–Free Cook: Gluten–Free Recipes for Everyone

GLUTEN-FREE ITALIAN

Over 150 Irresistible Recipes Without Wheat—from Crostini to Tiramisu

JACQUELINE MALLORCA

Da Capo
∞
LIFE
LONG

A MEMBER OF THE PERSEUS BOOKS GROUP

Copyright © 2009 Jacqueline Mallorca
Photographs © 2009
Sara Remington and Judi Swinks

Designed by Pauline Neuwirth
Set in 11 point Whitman by the Perseus Books Group

First Da Capo Press edition 2009

Library of Congress Cataloging-in-Publication Data
Mallorca, Jacqueline.
    Gluten-free Italian : over 150 irresistible recipes without wheat-from crostini to
tiramisu / Jacqueline Mallorca.—1st Da Capo Press ed.
        p. cm.
    Includes index.
    ISBN 978-0-7382-1361-3 (alk. paper)
    1. Gluten-free diet. 2. Gluten-free diet—Recipes. I. Title.
    RM237.86.M345 2009
    641.5'638—dc22

                                                            2009017600

Published by Da Capo Press
A Member of the Perseus Books Group
www.dacapopress.com

Note: The information in this book is true and complete to the best of our knowledge. This book is intended only as an informative guide for those wishing to know more about health issues. In no way is this book intended to replace, countermand, or conflict with the advice given to you by your own physician. The ultimate decision concerning care should be made between you and your doctor. We strongly recommend you follow his or her advice. Information in this book is general and is offered with no guarantees on the part of the authors or Da Capo Press. The author and publisher disclaim all liability in connection with the use of this book.

Da Capo Press books are available at special discounts for bulk purchases in the United States by corporations, institutions, and other organizations. For more information, please contact the Special Markets Department at the Perseus Books Group, 2300 Chestnut Street, Suite 200, Philadelphia, PA, 19103, or call (800) 810–4145, ext. 5000, or e-mail special.markets@perseusbooks.com.

10 9 8 7 6 5 4 3 2 1

To the memory of Elizabeth David,
who, for many of us, is the twentieth century's
single most influential and scholarly
food writer in the English language.

acknowledgments

Cookbooks don't spring fully formed from the foreheads of their authors, at least, not from mine. I couldn't have written *Gluten-Free Italian* without the support of my sterling literary agent Carole Bidnick, and my supportive, perceptive editor at Da Capo Press, Renée Sedliar.

My heartfelt gratitude goes also to Barbara Bochner, Alan Linder, Ginny Nile, Gail Reid, Inge Roberts, Anna Noelle Rockwell, Genevieve di San Faustino, Jill Sentz, and Mary Tonon. All these good friends and great cooks tirelessly tested and/or tasted recipes and offered insightful comments and encouragement.

In addition, I would like to express my warm appreciation to photographers Sara Remington and Judi Swinks, along with their respective food and prop stylists Kami Bremyer, Erin Quon, and Nani Steele. Their combined creativity and talent speak for themselves.

contents

introduction

Strictly speaking, there's no such thing as Italian food. The many different kingdoms in Italy were not unified under a centralized government until 1861, so instead of one basic Italian cuisine, there's traditional Ligurian food, Venetian food, Tuscan food, Sicilian food—in short, a wonderful array of regional specialties. What Italians do share is a huge respect for fresh, seasonal ingredients and an admirable, balanced attitude toward eating well.

I've been lucky enough to spend quite a bit of time exploring the foods of Italy firsthand, not in elegant hotels and restaurants but in trattorias and outdoor markets. Whatever was on offer during that first leisurely auto trip came as a revelation, from fragrant pesto-laced pasta in Genoa and Roman pizza bianco—so different from our American pizza—to Arabic-inspired desserts in Sicily, I loved it all. Who wouldn't?

Back in San Francisco, my love affair with Italian cooking continued unabated, conveniently fueled by all the Italian delicatessens in North Beach founded by early immigrants and the plethora of locally produced old-world salami, olive oil, artisanal cheese, wine, and glorious produce. One thing led to another, and I became a food writer, with many return trips to Europe.

Much to my chagrin, after coauthoring several cookbooks—including one on French pâtisserie and another on bread baking—I discovered that I was a food writer with celiac disease. I could no longer eat anything that contained wheat, barley, or rye. As I had absolutely no intention of giving up good food, I acquired a lot of funny flours and set to work.

This book doesn't pretend to be an all-encompassing volume of regional Italian cuisine. Instead, my main focus is on contemporary dishes that anyone who must avoid gluten would otherwise have to pass up: savory crostini and bruschetta; Mediterranean veggies with wonderful stuffings or toppings that involve bread crumbs; fresh ravioli and cannelloni; poultry, fish, and meat dishes that use a little flour in one form or another; crusty breads; and delectable desserts.

We share our lives with family and friends who are not gluten-intolerant, so the recipes are designed to please everyone at the table. They're based primarily on produce, alternative whole grains, olive oil, nuts, dairy products and eggs, augmented with poultry, fish, and meat. However, we live in the real world. Celiacs, like everyone else, sometimes run out of time and energy, so I've included a number of satisfying "off the shelf" recipes that are extra quick to prepare.

A traditional meal in Italy consists of several small courses, starting with an antipasto (this can be one dish or a selection of appetizers). The first course, or primo, can be pasta, risotto, or soup. Next comes a secondo of meat, poultry, or fish. This is accompanied by one or two vegetable side dishes and often followed by a green salad. Bread and wine always appear on the table. Finally, there's dessert, dolci, which at home is nearly always fresh fruit. Sweets are usually reserved for special occasions.

But times are changing. Today, people eat more lightly on a day-to-day basis, though with no less care and attention. Dinner might start with a vegetable appetizer followed by a meat course with one side dish and then fruit, or minestrone followed by salad and cheese. A glass of wine adds to the enjoyment and provides nature's own stress remedy.

Happily for those of us with celiac disease or a wheat allergy, there isn't a reason in the world why the gluten-challenged can't enjoy great food in true Italian style and continue to share the pleasures of the table with family and friends. After all, sharing a good meal is what keeps our relationships as well as our bodies alive and well.

If you are not already familiar with "going gluten-free," the thought of reinventing yourself as a gluten-free cook (or as a cook at all!) can be intimidating, so I've included a brief gluten-free shopper's guide, a description of all the gluten-free grains and flours generally available here—don't worry, I use only a few of the best-tasting and most versatile ones—an Italian ingredient glossary, and lots of cooking tips and product recommendations. You'll also find a list of useful celiac resources and mail order suppliers of gluten-free groceries at the back of the book.

Feel free to mix and match the following recipes in any order you please and use them as a springboard for your own healthful, tasty, gluten-free creations. It is my hope that those who are new to gluten-free cooking will make life-changing discoveries in these pages, and that experienced gluten-free cooks will find new inspiration. Buon appetito!

celiac disease—what is it?

It is estimated that over three million people in the United States have celiac disease, but of that number, many still remain undiagnosed or wrongly diagnosed. An autoimmune digestive disorder that wreaks havoc on the small intestine, it affects about 1 in every 133 Americans—and possibly many more.

A chronic inflammatory condition, celiac disease damages the villi, tiny fingerlike projections that cover innumerable small folds on the intestinal wall. These serve to massively increase the surface area of the small intestine to ensure efficient, rapid absorption of nutrients. Without healthy villi, a person becomes malnourished, regardless of how much they eat. This can lead to anything from porous bones or infertility to lymphatic cancer. Celiac disease is associated with other serious medical conditions, including lupus, Type 1 diabetes, rheumatoid arthritis, colitis, and thyroid disease.

Celiac disease can become active at any age, from childhood onward. It can lie dormant for years (or exhibit fairly minor symptoms that were assumed to be normal by the individual concerned) but be triggered by surgery, pregnancy, childbirth, viral infection, or even severe emotional distress. It is a difficult disease to diagnose as the symptoms vary so much from one person to the next and are often mistaken for being signs of other conditions. Thankfully, awareness is now growing, both among physicians and within the general public. Not so long ago, it took an average of eleven years to get a correct diagnosis.

What are the symptoms? Many people complain of diarrhea, gas, bloating, and abdominal pain. Malabsorption can cause weight loss, weakness, and poor growth in children. Celiac disease can also manifest itself in the form of an itchy, weepy skin condition called dermatitis herpetiformis. Clusters of small blisters persistently break out on the hands, inner elbows and knees, back, or scalp. This affects 15 to 25 percent of those with celiac disease, and although it does affect the gut, these people often have no digestive symptoms at all.

Unlike a food allergy, celiac disease is a genetic disorder; if one family member is diagnosed, near relatives should be tested as they're 22 percent more likely to have the celiac gene, too, even if they don't display any symptoms. To arrive at a diagnosis, if a simple blood test reveals certain antibodies, it will be followed by an intestinal biopsy.

Although there is currently no cure, the good news is that the disease can be controlled by scrupulously avoiding gluten, a protein found only in wheat, barley, and rye. Over time, the small intestine heals and symptoms disappear in almost all cases.

Avoiding gluten is no easy task because although most raw ingredients are naturally gluten-free, gluten is found in the form of wheat flour in so many processed and packaged foods, and of course fast foods and take-out items. Happily, food labeling has come a long way in the last few years. In 2006, the Food and Drug Administration mandated that any products containing wheat/gluten, milk, soy, peanuts, shellfish, and eggs should be so labeled. A flood of new gluten-free foods enters the market each year, and products have improved a great deal in flavor and texture. There was a time when the box tasted better than the gluten-free cookies it contained.

Thanks to the rising awareness of celiac disease, gluten-free groceries are now generally available in natural foods stores, major supermarkets, and online. Dedicated gluten-free bakeries have sprung up all over the country, and many restaurants now offer gluten-free options.

This is heartening for the millions of us with celiac disease, as well as an estimated additional seven million Americans who have a less serious but no less restrictive wheat intolerance or allergy.

But when all is said and done, the best way to avoid gluten in your food is to discover—or rediscover—the joys and satisfactions of cooking fresh ingredients in your own kitchen. It's not only better for everyone's long-term health, whether gluten-challenged or not, but much kinder to your waistline and your wallet.

the gluten-free shopper

As I recommended in my previous cookbook, *The Wheat-Free Cook: Gluten-Free Recipes for Everyone*, when you're shopping for foods without wheat or gluten, keep in mind the following updated "Yes," "Maybe," and "No" lists.

Always read ingredient labels carefully, and remember that anything marked "wheat-free" doesn't necessarily mean gluten-free as it could contain rye or barley, especially in the form of malt flavoring. Also, be wary of cross-contamination: an open bin of brown rice flour right next to an open bin of whole wheat flour could spell trouble. Buy sealed packages of gluten-free flours from suppliers such as Arrowhead Mills and Bob's Red Mill instead.

For mail-order suppliers of gluten-free groceries and useful contact information for celiac support groups and other resources, see page 217.

yes

- All fresh meats, seafood, poultry, and eggs; fish canned in oil, brine, or water; cured or cooked meats like prosciutto, pancetta, and ham; and many fresh and dried sausages. (Check the labels for any gluten-containing additions, like bread crumb fillers.)

- All fruits and vegetables (fresh, frozen, or canned), pure fruit juices; fresh and dried herbs; tomato purée and paste; dried beans, peas, and lentils; olives.

- All unflavored dairy products, including milk, cream, sour cream, cottage cheese, butter, and yogurt. (Check flavored cottage cheese and yogurt labels for any gluten-containing additions.)

- All types of cheese (except processed), such as Parmesan, ricotta, Swiss, blue, cheddar, and goat's and sheep's milk cheeses.

- Olive oil, canola oil, grape seed oil, and other pure vegetable oils; margarine.

- All vinegars (except malt vinegar).

- Chicken, beef, and vegetable broths, if labels reveal no wheat or hydrolyzed wheat protein.

- Jams and jellies, honey, sugar (brown, white, and confectioners'), molasses, maple syrup, and corn syrup.

- Plain chocolate (dark, milk, and white) and chocolate chips; pure cocoa powder.

- Plain nuts and nut flours; peanut butter.

- Tea, coffee, and pure hot chocolate and cocoa.

- Plain ice creams and frozen yogurts (no cookie crumb additions!) and sorbets.

- Rice (all types: white, brown, converted, Arborio, Jasmine, Basmati, etc.).

- Corn (cornmeal, polenta, precooked polenta rolls, masa harina, grits, cornstarch, tortillas, etc.).

- Gluten-free grains, seeds, and roots: amaranth, arrowroot, buckwheat (kasha), flax, millet, modified food starch (in the United States, it's made from corn), modified tapioca starch (trade name: Expandex), potato starch, potato flour, quinoa, sorghum, soy, tapioca (manioc), and teff.

- Pasta made from rice, corn, buckwheat, quinoa, amaranth, potato, bean, or chickpea flours; mung bean and Asian rice noodles.

- Miscellaneous ingredients:
    Annatto; citric acid, caramel, caramel coloring, and glucose syrup (in the United States they are derived from corn), malic and lactic acids; maltodextrin (a corn derivative, unrelated to barley malt); plain spices; sucrose, dextrose, and lactose; baking powder, baking soda, and cream of tartar; wheat-free tamari

yes   sauce or soy sauce; whole vanilla beans and pure vanilla extract; active dry yeast; guar gum and xanthan gum.

■ Wine (red, white, and rosé), and all distilled alcoholic beverages such as brandy, rum, Scotch, tequila, and vodka, as any gluten molecules present are too large to pass through the distillation process. Fortified wines such as Sherry, Port, and Madeira simply contain additional alcohol, so they are fine, too.

maybe   ■ Oats are technically gluten-free but may be contaminated with other grains during growing or processing. Buy oats that are labeled gluten-free. (Note that a few people cannot tolerate oats, gluten-free or not. Check with your physician.)

■ Mustards, ketchups, and salad dressings are usually free of gluten, but always check the labels for wheat-derived ingredients.

■ Pharmaceuticals and beauty products such as lipstick that might be ingested are usually gluten-free, but always check labels for wheat-derived products to make sure. Contact the manufacturer or your pharmacist if in doubt.

no   ■ Wheat, anything with wheat in its name except buckwheat (a misnomer; it is gluten-free), and any form of wheat such as bulgur, bread flour, cake flour, couscous, durum, einkorn, emmer, farina, farro, kamut, matzo, matzah, semolina, spelt, triticale, and wheat bran.

■ Bread, pizza, hamburger buns, cookies, crackers, pretzels, cakes, pastries, and other bakery items made from wheat, barley, or rye flour.

■ Breakfast cereals (except those marked gluten-free). Even standard cornflakes contain malt flavoring, which is made from barley. The vast majority of popular cereals, granolas, and "breakfast bars" are created from wheat or wheat blends.

■ Pasta made from wheat or semolina.

■ Foods containing hydrolized wheat protein, malt (flavoring, syrup, or extract), and malt vinegar, as malt is made from barley. (Note that maltodextrin, a sweetener, is made from corn and is therefore a "safe" item.)

- Ostensibly gluten-free foods that have been deep-fried in fat or cooked on a griddle that is also used for cooking foods that do contain gluten, as cross-contact from particles will occur.

- Meat, poultry, seafood, or vegetables that have been breaded, floured, are served with a sauce or gravy thickened with wheat flour, or marinated in a mixture that contains soy sauce or teriyaki sauce. This includes most frozen meals, fast foods, snack foods, and deli take-out items.

- Canned soups and chicken, beef, and vegetable broths containing flour or hydrolized wheat protein. Regular (as opposed to wheat-free) soy sauce, as it's brewed with a mixture of wheat and soy.

- Beer, as it is brewed from barley. However, good-tasting gluten-free beers made in the United States, Canada, Britain, and Australia are now available.

MULTIPLE-ALLERGY SUBSTITUTIONS

SOME PEOPLE WITH celiac disease have to cope with multiple food allergies. There are eight major food allergens: wheat, milk, eggs, peanuts, tree nuts, fish, shellfish, and soy. Try these substitutions (in equal amounts) if any of these foods present additional problems.

Milk: Use soy milk, coconut milk, or rice milk plus 1 egg yolk in every 8-ounce cupful.

Yogurt: Use soy yogurt.

Butter: Use Fleischmann's unsalted margarine, Earth Balance Buttery Spread (nondairy), or Spectrum Organic Shortening.

Eggs: For less than two eggs, called for in baking, you can use 1 tablespoon flaxmeal plus 3 tablespoons water per large egg (let stand until thick, stirring now and then, about 10 minutes). Otherwise, use Egg Replacer according to package directions, but be aware that if you are replacing more than two eggs, the recipe may be compromised.

Tree nuts and peanuts: Use pumpkin seeds, sunflower seeds, or toasted coconut.

Peanut butter: Use almond butter or make your own hazelnut butter in a food processor.

---

gluten-free grains, flours, and other baking ingredients

D on't be alarmed by the length of this list, which has been updated from the collection of alternative flours listed in my
previous cookbook, *The Wheat-Free Cook: Gluten-Free Recipes for
Everyone*, to include newly available products. You don't need them
all—far from it—but it's good to know that they exist should you
need to make substitutions to suit your own needs or preferences.

**ALMOND MEAL/
FLOUR**
Usually ground from unpeeled almonds, this mellow, off-white,
high-protein flour is available ready-ground, but unless you can
find a source with a high turnover (to insure freshness) and rea-
sonable prices, it's best to grind your own. Use a hand-cranked
nut mill or an electric coffee mill reserved for grinding items
other than coffee. If using a food processor, combine the whole
almonds listed in a recipe with 2 tablespoons of rice flour or sugar
subtracted from the other ingredients. This helps to prevent turning the nuts into paste by mistake. Store almond meal in the
freezer for up to six months.

AMARANTH
A tiny round grain known as the Mother Grain in the Inca em-
pire, *Amaranthus caudatus* is not a true cereal, though it's used
like one. High in protein, calcium, iron, and fiber, the whole
grains cook in 15 minutes or less. The flour has a slightly astrin-
gent taste, so use no more than 15 percent in a flour blend.

ARROWROOT
Derived from the rootlike rhizomes of various tropical plants and
generally used as a thickener, this white starch gives a silky finish

to sauces. Be cautious about utilizing it in a cookie dough, as too much will turn baked cookies into cement.

Bean, chickpea, lentil, and soy flour are high in protein, fiber, and calcium but have quite pronounced flavors. Garfava flour is a proprietary blend of garbanzo, fava, and romana bean flour. In general, bean flours are best used in small amounts in flour blends for gluten-free breads.

BEAN (LEGUME) FLOUR

Not wheat at all but a relative of rhubarb—the name is derived from the Dutch *bockweit* as these triangular seeds were thought to resemble beechnuts—buckwheat is a hardy plant that manages to flourish in poor soils and inhospitable climates. Famously used in Russian blini (pancakes) and Japanese soba noodles, a little buckwheat flour imparts a rustic, "whole-grain" flavor to gluten-free breads.

BUCKWHEAT

The European chestnut, *Castanea sativa*, contains more starch and far less oil than any other tree nut and makes a distinctive, sweet-tasting flour. (Don't confuse European chestnuts with Asian water chestnuts, which are not tree nuts but rootlike rhizomes.) Italian cooks use chestnut flour in pasta, polenta, and bakery items.

CHESTNUT FLOUR

A favorite baking ingredient, chocolate is derived from the seeds of cacao trees. Depending on where they're grown, cacao beans, like coffee beans, have distinct flavor characteristics: fruity, floral, and so on. After harvesting, the beans undergo fermentation, when they start to develop their unique flavors, and are then dried and graded. Chocolate manufacturers roast and hull the beans to free the meat, or nibs. The cacao nibs are ground into a thick paste of cacao butter and vegetable solids.

CHOCOLATE

Unsweetened chocolate is essentially smooth, solidified chocolate paste with a high percentage of cacao butter. Bittersweet, semisweet, and milk chocolate contains increasing amounts of sugar, so the percentage of cacao butter decreases accordingly. White chocolate is cacao butter (often mixed with some other, cheaper fat) combined with lots of sugar, milk solids, and vanilla.

COCOA Cocoa powder can be used like flour for chocolate cakes. It's made after the chocolate paste is pressed to extract most of its cacao butter. The remaining solids are made into unsweetened natural or Dutch processed cocoa powder. Natural cocoa powder gives a deep, intense chocolate flavor to baked goods and is the form I prefer. Dutch processed cocoa is treated with an alkali to neutralize its natural acidity; it has a more delicate flavor and dissolves easily in liquids.

COCONUT FLOUR This fragrant, low-carb, high-fiber flour is especially useful for those with multiple food sensitivities as it's widely tolerated. In a flour blend, 15 percent is about right for most palates.

CORN FLOUR, CORNMEAL, AND CORNSTARCH Corn, more often known outside the United States as maize, is actually a kind of grass with huge seed heads or cobs.

Finely ground corn flour is useful for breads, cakes, and cookies. Coarse, medium, and finely ground cornmeal is used mainly for Italian polenta, American cornbread, and grits. (Cornmeal can be ground finer in a clean coffee mill to make corn flour.) If possible, avoid labels that say "degerminated" when buying corn products; you want the whole, stone-ground grain. It's not only more healthful but has a wonderful flavor.

Cornstarch is a silky white powder with no nutritional value, but it's useful in gluten-free baking as it helps to smooth out the slightly granular texture of many gluten-free flours. When used as thickener for sauces, cornstarch adds a silky finish.

FLAX SEEDS, FLAXMEAL According to nutritionists, flax seeds are one of the most nutritious plant foods on the planet. They contain more heart-healthy omega-3 oil than fish and more fiber than oats, and they supply protein. Fortunately, they also have a pleasantly nutty, grassy flavor. You can grind your own using an electric coffee mill (a food processor just spins them around as the outer coating is extremely hard), or buy preground flaxmeal and store it for up to six months in the freezer. (Whole flax seeds keep at room temperature for at least a year.) Using a little flaxmeal in a flour blend lends suppleness as well as goodness to gluten-free breads as it's high in flax oil.

Derived from by-products of wine making, these varietal-specific flours (American-grown Chardonnay, Riesling, Cabernet, and Merlot) are high in antioxidants and contain the health benefits of wine such as omega-3 and -6, potassium, vitamin A, and iron. Used with a light hand, they add color and flavor to anything from chocolate cake or meat sauces to homemade egg pasta.

GRAPE SEED FLOURS

Made from the seeds of a beanlike plant, guar gum is high in soluble fiber and works well as a binder in gluten-free bread baking, preventing dryness and crumbling. Interchangeable with xanthan gum in equal amounts, it costs less.

Be aware that in some individuals guar gum can have a laxative effect.

GUAR GUM

One of the first grains to be cultivated by humankind, about 12,000 years ago, nutritious millet contains almost 15 percent protein. It has a mellow, nutty flavor and cooks in just 15 minutes, but few people in the United States are familiar with it. Top-grade millet (not birdseed millet) makes a good pilaf or grain salad, especially when toasted before using. Use up to 20 percent millet flour in gluten-free flour blends for breads.

MILLET, MILLET FLOUR

A storehouse of vitamins, minerals, and fiber as well as being good to eat at any time, almonds, hazelnuts, pecans, and walnuts make luxurious gluten-free flours. True, most nuts are also high in oil, but it's the heart-healthy, mono- or polyunsaturated kind. When nuts are ground, the flavorful oil content can take the place of other fats in baking, just as the starchy part stands in for flour. (Peanuts are not true nuts but legumes, but they are treated like tree nuts.) Store shelled nuts and nut flours in the freezer for up to six months. Dried nuts in the shell will keep at room temperature for two weeks, or up to one year in the refrigerator.

NUTS, NUT FLOURS

Nutritious, fiber-rich oats do not contain gluten, despite rumors to the contrary. However, oats are particularly subject to cross-contamination by other grains in the field, and/or during the milling and packing process in facilities that also handle wheat. Happily, several American companies now produce certified gluten-free oatmeal and oat flour. (You can grind oatmeal flakes

OATS, OAT FLOUR, OATMEAL

OATS, OAT FLOUR, OATMEAL (cont.)	in a clean coffee mill to make your own oat flour for bread.) Note that a few individuals cannot tolerate oats, gluten-free or not. Consult your physician if in doubt.
POTATO FLOUR	Made from dehydrated potatoes, this cream-colored flour is high in protein and fiber but has a pronounced flavor. Potato flour is best used in small amounts with other gluten-free flours for bread making; don't confuse it with potato starch, which is much lighter.
POTATO STARCH	Made from the starchy content of dehydrated potatoes, this silky white powder has no nutritional value but is invaluable in gluten-free baking as part of a gluten-free blend. It aids lightness and smoothes out the texture of coarser flours.
QUINOA, QUINOA FLAKES, QUINOA FLOUR	Along with amaranth, high-protein quinoa helped to sustain the vast Inca empire before the arrival of the Spanish conquerors, who banned its cultivation for religious and political reasons. Botanically a relative of Swiss chard and beets, the whole grains make excellent pilafs and hearty salads. Most whole quinoa must be rinsed before cooking to remove the residue of bitter saponins, the plant's defense against insects.
	Quinoa flakes make a mellow, high-protein addition to stuffings and meat loaves and can be cooked like oatmeal for breakfast.
	Quinoa flour, used in amounts of up to 20 percent with other gluten-free flours, lends nutrition and a nutty flavor to rustic-style breads.
RICE, RICE FLOUR	Rice, *oryza sativa*, sustains over half the world's population. There are hundreds of varieties, but all of them fall into two main categories: *Indica* rice, with grains that cook dry and separate, and *Japonica* rice that sticks together.
	Whole, or brown rice, contains complex carbohydrates, thiamin, riboflavin, niacin, phosphorus, iron, potassium, and fiber. White rice is refined, with the germ and bran removed. Converted rice is parboiled before refining, a process that forces some of the B vitamins into the endosperm so they are not lost when the bran is polished off, but it's still not as healthful as brown rice. All kinds of rice (except most of the flavored packaged varieties) are gluten-free.

The all-purpose workhorse of the gluten-free kitchen, flour milled from rice is mellow in flavor. When used in baking, both brown and white rice flour are best combined with cornstarch, potato starch, or tapioca starch to counteract the slightly coarse texture.

Short-grained Asian glutinous (spelled with an "i") rice is another term for sweet, sticky, or mochi rice. It does not contain gluten. Flour made from it is extremely sticky when cooked, as you will discover if you have ever tried Japanese mochi cakes or buns.

An essential nutrient, our bodies all need some sodium (salt) to function properly. Sea salt is much preferred in cooking by professional chefs for its more delicate flavor. Harvested from evaporated seawater, it contains useful trace minerals, including some naturally occurring iodine. Packed in tall blue cans, Baleine sea salt from France is widely available and fine for general cooking, as is neutral-tasting pure kosher salt, which is usually rock salt.

Rock salt is mined from mineral deposits and refined to produce pure sodium chloride. Iodized salt is rock salt fortified with iodine and has a noticeably metallic flavor. (Taste sea salt and iodized table salt side by side to experience the flavor difference. You will be amazed.)

Essential for proper thyroid function, which plays a vital role in the regulation of growth and energy expenditure, iodine is necessary for human survival. Historically, it has been added to table salt to combat iodine deficiencies—once a problem in inland areas—but these days iodine is available to us from many different sources, including seafood, nori, dairy products, and produce grown in iodine-rich soil.

There's just one caveat for celiacs. Iodine does not contain gluten, but it can worsen the rash in celiacs with dermatitis herpetiformis, so it's advisable to temporarily avoid both iodized salt and even sea salt due to the tiny amount of iodine it may naturally contain. (Season food with plain kosher salt instead.) However, when the rash has cleared up completely after following a gluten-free diet, ingesting iodine should no longer present a problem.

SALT

SORGHUM (MILO) FLOUR

High in protein, fiber, and several vitamins, sorghum flour has a slightly sweet taste and lends a darker color than many other gluten-free flours to bakery items, so it's best for rustic-style breads and gingerbread. Use up to 25 percent sorghum in a flour blend.

TAPIOCA STARCH/FLOUR

A favorite for bread baking when combined with other gluten-free flours, tapioca starch (also marketed as tapioca flour) lends a desirable chewy, slightly elastic quality. Made from the root of the cassava (manioc) plant, it looks like cornstarch and can also be used as a thickener for gravies and sauces. Modified tapioca starch (trade name: Expandex) acts as a binder in baking blends, but use no more than 10 percent in relation to other flours.

TEFF, TEFF FLOUR

The staple grain of Ethiopia and Eritrea, this tiny, highly nutritious grain is now cultivated successfully in the United States. Available as ivory-colored flour at natural foods stores and by mail order, teff has a pleasant, slightly molasses-like flavor. Useful for baking, it also makes an outstanding ingredient for Italian gnocchi. A form of millet, teff is high in iron, calcium, minerals, protein, and dietary fiber and contains all eight essential amino acids, making it an exceptional nutritional bargain.

WILD RICE

Not a true rice at all, brown-hulled wild rice is the long-grained, slightly smoky-flavored seed of an aquatic grass. Indigenous to the Great Lakes region, this luxury item is usually blended with various types of rice because of its high price. Wild rice has a delicious, woodsy flavor and twice the protein and fiber of brown rice but not as much iron and calcium.

XANTHAN GUM

A white powder derived from corn sugar, xanthan gum is used extensively in the food industry as a binder. Invaluable when baking with gluten-free flours as it prevents dryness and crumbling, very small amounts also benefit homemade pasta, tart dough, and some cakes and cookies that can otherwise be too fragile. Interchangeable with guar gum, some bakers like to use half of each in a given recipe. Both these products must be measured carefully, as too much of a good thing will impart a slippery or ropy texture.

the naturally gluten-free italian pantry

These tiny saltwater fish from the Mediterranean and southern Atlantic, related to sardines, are eaten fresh or preserved in salt or oil. Imported anchovies packed in olive oil are the most widely available, but those packed in salt have the best texture and flavor. Packed in 2-pound flat cans, they can be bought "loose" in Italian delicatessens and some large supermarkets. For convenience, the recipes in this book call for canned anchovies, but substitute the salt-cured kind if you prefer. Anchovy paste in tubes is the least desirable but will do in a pinch.

ANCHOVIES

To fillet salt-cured anchovies, rinse off the salt and split them open with a sharp knife. Lift off the backbone, which looks just like a zipper and comes off readily in one piece. Also discard the tail and any scratchy bits you can feel with your fingers. You'll be left with two meaty "sides" with superior texture and flavor.

An Italian condiment of ancient lineage made from unfermented, cooked white Trebbiano grape juice, the best (and very expensive) ones are aged for at least 12 years in a complex process. As the liquid evaporates, it's transferred to smaller and smaller barrels of different aromatic woods, gradually becoming infinitely richer, darker, and more syrupy. The real thing is made only in Emilia-Romagna, in either Modena or certain parts of Reggio, and must be approved by a consortium of tasters before it can be bottled as *tradizionale*. A two-year-old one is fine for cooking, but beware the mass-market (read, suspiciously inexpensive) kind, as you're paying for nicely packaged vinegar with a good dollop of caramel coloring.

BALSAMICO/ BALSAMIC VINEGAR

CAPERS/
CAPER BERRIES
The unopened buds of a flowering shrub, *Capparis soinosa*, which grows wild all over the Mediterranean, capers are usually sold packed in vinegar, brine, or salt.

Capers packed in salt have the most flavor. If left on the bush, caper buds develop into berries like tiny rose hips, which are also sold salted or pickled and make a great garnish.

CHEESES
Italy produces a huge array of traditional, hand-crafted cheeses in its various regions that easily rival—and dare I say often outdo—those of France. The best known are now usually available in upscale American supermarkets, Italian delis, and specialty cheese shops. The real McCoy all have a DOC (for *Denominazione di Origine Controllata*, or "name and origin controlled") designation on the label. They're wonderful eaten with gluten-free bread or crackers; many are also utilized in cooking. Buy good cheese in small quantities, so it remains perfect down to the last morsel.

Fontina Valle D'Aosta: A classic, semi-firm, raw cow's milk cheese from Piedmont with nutty, herbacious notes, it melts beautifully. You can substitute Swiss-made Gruyère in cooking. (Scandinavian-made Fontina in the red wax rind is very bland.)

Gorgonzola: Lombardy's pride and joy, Gorgonzola is made in two versions, the younger *dolce* (sweet) and the more mature *naturale* (sharp). Years ago, this superb cow's milk cheese got its greenish-blue striations from a beneficial mold that occurs naturally in damp caves. However, during the last forty-plus years, Gorgonzola cheese has instead been pierced with copper or stainless steel needles to introduce a commercially produced version called *Penicillium gorgonzola*. (Today, virtually all commercially produced blue cheeses are injected in this way.)

Mascarpone: Like ricotta, mascarpone is more of a dairy product than a cheese as no rennet is used to make it. Made from the partly drained cream of cow's milk, this sublimely rich, semi-solid cream has a butterfat content of about 70 percent. Now made and widely available in the United States, it adds incomparable flavor and texture to desserts such as Tiramisu and Zuppe Inglese.

Mozzarella: Originally made from the milk of water buffalo, delicate white Mozzarella *di bufala* remains the best, though the Italians do make lots of cheaper cow's milk mozzarella, too. Fresh buffalo mozzarella is moist and milky, with a springy texture, and has a buttery, nutty flavor. American supermarket mozzarella, by contrast, is tasteless and extremely rubbery. For topping pizza, I much prefer to use sliced or grated Fontina or Gruyère cheese.

Parmigiano-Reggiano (Parmesan): The undisputed king of cheeses, Parmesan pretty much underpins Italian cuisine. It does miraculous things for all sorts of vegetables and fruits from spinach gnocchi to ripe pears and, of course, pasta, polenta, and risotto dishes.

Genuine Parmesan is a *grana*, a granular hard cheese with a matchless flavor and crystalline texture. It grates into fine grains or flakes that melt in the mouth. Much copied, the genuine article is labeled "Parmigiano-Reggiano." For full enjoyment, always grate your own. Once you've tasted freshly grated genuine Parmesan, you'll never go back to those shiny green shaker cans. Grana Padana, a less expensive cousin, is a worthwhile alternative, as is aged Bear Flag Brand Dry Jack from the Vella Cheese Company of California. (Founded in 1931, this Italian family-run company's artisanal cheeses are excellent.)

Pecorino Romano (Pecorino): A salty, sharp-tasting, sheep's milk grating cheese, the finest pecorino is Pecorino Romano, made in the province of Rome, but good-quality pecorino also comes from the island of Sardinia under the name Pecorino Sardo. Traditionally, pecorino is the preferred grating cheese in southern Italy; Parmesan is favored in the north.

Ricotta: As with mascarpone, ricotta is technically a dairy product, not a cheese. In Italy, it's made mostly from the whey of sheep's milk. In the United States, ricotta is usually made from the whey of cow's milk. American ricotta is more bland and far more moist.

Taleggio: A voluptuous cow's milk table cheese from Lombardy, Taleggio bulges gently when it's fully ripened. Sublimely rich and buttery, it has a full, rounded, complex flavor that's complemented by fresh fruit, particularly ripe pears.

COPPA Somewhat like prosciutto, coppa (or capicolla) is made from cuts of pork neck or shoulder meat rather than the hind leg. As with prosciutto, it's usually served as an antipasto, in very thin slices. To produce it, the meat is marinated in wine with salt and spices, compressed into a sausage shape, and air dried for up to six months. Available in mild and hot versions, coppa is sliced to order in Italian delis and can be found in some markets presliced and vacuum packed.

OLIVES A staple of the Mediterranean diet for thousands of years, all olives start off green and slowly ripen to brownish-purple or black. Unlike the insipid canned black olives that support the California olive industry, Mediterranean olives are very flavorful and undergo an entirely different curing process. There are hundreds of different varieties, but widely available large green Sicilian olives, oil-cured black olives, and brownish Kalamata olives (similar to Italian Gaeta olives) are used for the recipes in this book.

OLIVE OIL Olive oil is simply the minimally processed juice of an oil-rich fruit. Graded according to acidity levels, extra-virgin olive oil has the lowest, coupled with the purest, fruitiest flavor. The best and most expensive are estate bottled—meaning the olives were grown, harvested, crushed for oil, and bottled on the same estate. Such fine oils are best reserved for dressing salads and vegetables; cooking with them would destroy some of the flavor notes. Extra-virgin cold-pressed olive oils from less famous producers—especially those from Greece, Australia, and northern California—offer good value for far less money. It's fine to use these more affordable oils for both cooking and drizzling purposes. Taste several over time to discover whether you prefer a peppery, herbaceous, or mellow, buttery flavor. Whatever olive oil you choose, store it at room temperature but shield the bottle from light and heat, as both will cause this natural, minimally processed oil to become rancid.

PANCETTA Pancetta is unsmoked Italian bacon and comes from the same cut of pork belly as American bacon but has a far less aggressive flavor. It's usually cured with nothing more than salt and black pepper and tightly rolled into a fat sausage shape. It can be sliced to order and keeps refrigerated for a few days, or purchase it sliced or diced in convenient plastic packs. Unopened, these have a conveniently long refrigerator shelf life of several weeks.

Dried gluten-free pasta is now widely available in American natural foods stores, many large supermarkets, and by mail order (see page 217 for purveyors). Made from a variety of alternative flours—mainly rice, corn, and quinoa—manufacturers package a number of the best-known shapes, including spaghetti, fettuccine, penne, spirals, lasagne, and shells.

PASTA, GLUTEN-FREE VARIETIES

Polenta is ground cornmeal cooked in water, broth, or milk to make a form of porridge that's served with cheese, vegetables, meat, or seafood. When cooled, it sets into a firm shape that can be sliced for broiling or baking with various sauces. Coarse-grain raw cornmeal can take up to an hour to cook, which is why many Italian cooks now use instant or fine-grain cornmeal for everyday home cooking. Precooked polenta is available in shelf-stable rolls in American supermarkets. It will do in a pinch but lacks texture and flavor.

POLENTA/CORNMEAL

The concentrated, woodsy fragrance of dried porcini (boletus mushrooms) can turn domestic mushrooms into a magnificent sauce for polenta, pasta, or risotto. You don't need much, which is just as well as they're expensive. When buying dried porcini, look for large, creamy-brown slices, not the dark, crumbly kind. Always save the aromatic soaking liquid for sauces and soups. Stored airtight, dried porcini will last almost indefinitely.

PORCINI, DRIED

Prosciutto is actually the Italian word for ham. *Prosciutto cotto* is cooked ham; *prosciutto crudo* denotes the paper-thin, rosy pink slices of air-dried, slightly salty yet sweet-tasting raw ham that we all know and love. The latter is undoubtedly the most noble end to which a pig's hind leg can aspire and takes a great deal of skill and patience to produce. The best comes from Parma and Friuli (San Daniele) and is widely distributed in the United States. For cooking, I watch for half-priced stubby "ends" of prosciutto and chop and freeze the meat. Look for these bargains only in delis with a high turnover, so the prosciutto is not stale.

PROSCIUTTO

RISOTTO RICE The three Italian rice varieties most often used for risotto—Arborio, Carnaroli, and Vialone Nano—share unique characteristics: the round, short grains can absorb lots of flavorful broth without losing their shape, yet retain a faint bite in the center. Stirring this kind of rice as it cooks helps to release the starch, which gives the finished risotto a wonderfully creamy texture.

TOMATOES, CANNED Sun-ripened, flavorful tomatoes, essential in so many Italian dishes, are strictly seasonal, so like everyone else, Italian cooks rely on good-quality canned tomatoes during the rest of the year. San Marzano plum tomatoes are favored for sauces. Cultivated in the rich, volcanic soil below Mt. Vesuvius, they're dense, sweet, and flavorful and packed in a delicious tomato purée. They're exported to the United States, as are plain and simple Italian Pomi brand chopped ripe tomatoes, which come in handy shelf-stable boxes. Though they're more expensive, it's worth trying imported San Marzano and Pomi brand tomatoes at least once, to use as a benchmark. Then sample different domestically grown and packed canned tomatoes until you find a brand that comes close in taste and texture. (Perhaps surprisingly, our canned tomatoes can vary wildly in quality, from good to something that resembles chopped boiled watermelon.)

contorni/
vegetable dishes

AN ITALIAN *CONTORNO*, a side dish or "border" for the
meat course, provides nutritional balance and color as
well as wonderful flavors. In practice, most of these versatile,
veggie-based dishes double as warm or room-temperature
appetizers and can become a main course when served in
larger portions.

For the gluten-challenged, health-minded cook, contorni
provide the best possible way to enjoy a huge variety of vegetables. Adding a little olive oil, a handful of crispy gluten-
free crumbs, and a few shavings of Parmesan makes all the
difference.

stuffed mushrooms with pancetta

Serve these mushrooms warm or at room temperature as an appetizer, or as an accompaniment for roast chicken or steak. Gluten-free bread crumbs absorb the flavorful juices and contribute to a satisfying texture.

SERVES 4 AS AN APPETIZER OR SIDE DISH

Preheat the oven to 375°F. Spray an 8 x 10-inch shallow baking dish lightly with olive oil.

Wipe the mushrooms with a damp paper towel. Remove and chop the stalks.

Arrange the mushroom caps in the baking dish, hollow side up.

Warm the olive oil in a skillet over moderate heat. Add the onion, garlic, chopped mushroom stalks, and pancetta. Sauté until softened, about 5 minutes.

Turn off the heat and stir in the parsley, bread crumbs, and Parmesan. Season the mixture with salt and pepper and spoon it into the mushroom caps. Don't worry if some crumbs fall into the dish.

Spray the mushrooms lightly with olive oil. Bake until tender and lightly browned on top, about 15 minutes. Serve warm or at room temperature.

Olive oil cooking spray

12 medium white mushrooms, about ¾ pound

2 tablespoons extra-virgin olive oil

2 tablespoons finely chopped yellow onion

1 garlic clove, chopped

3 tablespoons finely chopped pancetta or unsmoked bacon (salt pork)

2 tablespoons chopped flat-leaf parsley

¼ cup Homemade Bread Crumbs (page 163)

1 ounce (about ¼ cup) grated Parmigiano-Reggiano

Fine sea salt and freshly ground black pepper

BREAD CRUMBS

SO REVERED IN the Italian kitchen that it is never wasted, day-old bread is "recycled" into bread crumbs and used in countless ways. Happily, excellent gluten-free bread is easy to make—see Chapter 9—or you can utilize the interior of a commercially prepared, mellow, frozen gluten-free loaf with a light texture such as Glutino's Gluten Free Fiber Bread or Gluten Free Flax Bread. Be aware that most of the other loaves available in natural foods stores are too sweet and too highly flavored for use in savory dishes.

Soft, gluten-free bread crumbs are sometimes available commercially but are expensive, and gluten-free cracker crumbs—sometimes erroneously labeled as bread crumbs—are not sufficiently absorbent to take up good flavors and contribute the right texture. To prepare bread crumbs, see page 163.

stuffed zucchini boats

Good warm or at room temperature, these stuffed veggies make an attractive an-
tipasto or main dish. The best tool for scooping out the centers of the zucchini is a
curved, serrated grapefruit knife, but a carefully wielded teaspoon works, too.

SERVES 6 AS AN APPETIZER

3 small zucchini,
about 6 inches long

2 tablespoons
extra-virgin olive oil

2 tablespoons finely
chopped onion

1 garlic clove, chopped

2 tablespoons chopped
pancetta or unsmoked
bacon (salt pork)

Fine sea salt and freshly
ground black pepper

¼ cup Homemade
Bread Crumbs, plus 2
tablespoons (page 163)

1 ounce
(about ¼ cup) grated
Parmigiano-Reggiano

Olive oil spray

Preheat the oven to 375°F. Set out a shallow baking dish just large enough to hold the split zucchini in one layer.

Bring a large pot of water to a boil. Add the zucchini and parboil for 4 minutes.

Drain, and when cool enough to handle, slice in half lengthways. Scoop out the center pulp and reserve, leaving a ¼-inch thick shell, and chop the pulp.

Grease the baking dish with 1 tablespoon of the olive oil, and arrange the zucchini halves in it, hollow side up.

Warm the remaining tablespoon of olive oil in a skillet over medium-low heat. Add the onion, garlic, pancetta, and reserved zucchini pulp. Sauté, stirring, until the onion and zucchini pulp soften and turn translucent, about 7 minutes. Season to taste with salt and pepper. Remove from the heat, and stir in the ¼ cup bread crumbs and 2 tablespoons of the grated cheese.

Divide the filling among the zucchini halves, spooning it in lightly. (Don't tamp it down.) It's fine if a few crumbs fall into the dish. Top the filled zucchini with the remaining 2 tablespoons of bread crumbs and the Parmesan. Spray with olive oil. Cover the baking dish with aluminum foil, and bake for 15 minutes.

Remove the foil, and continue baking until the top surface is crispy and starting to turn brown, a further 15 to 20 minutes.

yellow peppers with anchovies, pine nuts, and raisins

These meltingly tender stuffed bell peppers have intriguing sweet and savory notes that make them very appetizing. The peppers are roasted first to caramelize them and loosen the skins, which can be done the day before if this is more convenient.

SERVES 4 TO 8 AS AN APPETIZER

Preheat the oven to 425°F. Line a rimmed baking sheet with aluminum foil, and spray an 8 x 10-inch shallow baking dish with olive oil.

Cut the peppers in half lengthwise. Cut out the stalks and ribs and discard the seeds. Arrange cut side down on the baking sheet. Bake until the skins look wrinkled and are starting to blacken in spots, about 25 minutes.

Remove from the oven, cover with more foil and let steam for 10 minutes. When the peppers are cool enough to handle, gently pull off the skins and any crispy blackened bits. The pepper halves will be soft. Arrange in the baking dish cut side up and supporting each other.

Reduce the oven heat to 375°F.

Place the anchovy fillets in a mixing bowl and chop finely. (This saves "aromatizing" a cutting board.) Add the bread crumbs, pine nuts, raisins, capers, olives, basil, and salt. Stir in the olive oil, and mix well.

Spoon the anchovy mixture into the pepper halves. Spray the tops with olive oil.

Bake until the stuffing is lightly golden, about 20 minutes. Serve warm or at room temperature.

Olive oil spray

4 medium yellow bell peppers, about 6 ounces each

4 canned anchovy fillets, drained

½ cup Homemade Bread Crumbs (page 163)

2 tablespoons pine nuts

2 tablespoons yellow raisins

2 teaspoons capers, rinsed and drained, chopped if large

8 Kalamata olives, drained, pitted, and chopped

3 tablespoons chopped basil or flat-leaf parsley

Pinch fine sea salt

3 tablespoons extra-virgin olive oil

stuffed tomatoes, sicilian style

Highlight the wonderful sweetness of vine-ripened tomatoes with the contrasting saltiness of anchovies and olives in this classic Italian recipe. Serve them at room temperature, as part of an antipasti selection, or warm, as a side dish.

SERVES 6 AS AN APPETIZER OR SIDE DISH

Olive oil spray

6 medium vine-ripened tomatoes, about 2¼-inch diameter

3 tablespoons extra-virgin olive oil

1 small onion, finely chopped

2 garlic cloves, chopped

4 canned anchovy fillets, lightly drained

1 tablespoon capers, drained and rinsed

12 pitted Kalamata olives, 6 chopped and 6 cut in half

2 teaspoons chopped fresh parsley

½ cup Homemade Bread Crumbs (page 163)

Preheat the oven to 350°F. Spray a shallow baking dish just large enough to hold the halved tomatoes in one layer lightly with olive oil.

Cut the tomatoes in half horizontally and scoop out and discard a little but not all of the center seeds and pulp. Place in the baking dish, cut side up.

Warm the olive oil in a small skillet over moderate heat and sauté the onion and garlic until softened but not colored, about 5 minutes. Remove from the heat.

Place the anchovy fillets in a mixing bowl and mash or chop finely. Add the capers, the chopped olives, parsley, and bread crumbs. Add the onion and garlic, and mix well.

Spoon the anchovy mixture into the tomatoes, and top each one with an olive half. Spray the tomatoes with olive oil and bake until the tomato skins begin to wrinkle, about 20 minutes. Serve warm or at room temperature.

OLIVE OIL SPRAY

SPRAYING OLIVE OIL over a dish as opposed to drizzling means that you use far less and distribute it evenly. (It's a "good" oil but still high in calories!) Pour your own oil into an opaque spray bottle designed for dispensing oil (light hastens the oxidation of olive oil) or buy olive oil cooking spray in a can.

stuffed tomatoes with risotto

Italian cooks are brilliant at making something good out of nothing very much: witness these tomatoes stuffed with creamy leftover risotto and pesto sauce and crowned with a crunchy topping.

Serves 4 as an appetizer

Preheat the oven to 375°F.

Cut the tomatoes in half horizontally and scoop out and discard most of the core and seeds.

Pour the olive oil into an 8 x 10 x 2-inch baking dish. Arrange the tomatoes in it, cut side up. Place a half teaspoon of pesto into each one and top with the risotto.

Grate the cheese over the filled tomatoes, and top with the bread crumbs, pressing them lightly into place. It's fine if some fall into the dish. Spray the tomatoes lightly with olive oil.

Bake until the tomatoes are tender and the skins start to wrinkle, about 20 minutes. Let cool for 10 minutes before serving. Spoon some of the browned juices and crumbs in the baking dish over each serving.

4 medium vine-ripened tomatoes, about 2¼-inch diameter

2 tablespoons olive oil

4 teaspoons Pesto Sauce (page 49), or from a jar

8 heaped tablespoons leftover risotto (see recipes in Chapter 4), cold

2 tablespoons grated Pecorino Romano or Parmigiano-Reggiano

2 tablespoons Homemade Bread Crumbs (page 163)

Olive oil spray

butternut squash and potato gratinato

This tender, golden side dish complements everything from roast lamb to the holiday turkey. Choose a butternut squash with a long neck, for making perfect slices that match the potato slices, and chop the flesh of the leftover base for use in soup.

SERVES 6 AS A SIDE DISH

1 butternut squash, 2 to 2½ pounds

1 pound medium to large waxy potatoes, such as Yukon Gold

4 tablespoons unsalted butter, cut in small dice, plus extra for baking dish

Fine sea salt and freshly ground black pepper

3 ounces (about 1 cup) shredded Fontina or Gruyère

2 tablespoons grated Parmigiano-Reggiano

1¼ cups gluten-free beef, chicken, or vegetable broth

Preheat the oven to 400°F.

Cut the neck off the squash, reserving the base for another use. Peel down to the bright orange flesh. Cut in half lengthways, and slice ⅛-inch thick (a handheld mandoline slicer will do this in no time).

Slice the peeled potatoes ⅛-inch thick and drop into a large bowl of cold water to rinse off the starch. Drain and pat dry on paper towels.

Grease an 8-cup shallow baking dish lightly with butter. Spread half the squash slices on the bottom, sprinkle with a little salt and a grinding of pepper and ¼ cup of the Fontina. Top with half the potato slices, salt and pepper, and ¼ cup of Parmesan. Dot with half the butter. Repeat the layers, ending with a topping of overlapped potato slices. Pour the broth around the edges, and sprinkle the surface with the Parmesan and butter bits.

Bake until the vegetables are tender (test with a knife) and surface is golden, about 45 minutes. Let cool for 10 minutes before cutting and serving.

TIP: Use a fresh butternut squash with a buff-colored, unblemished skin that feels heavy for its size, so that the neck is still solid and seedless. If one has been around in your kitchen for a while, as can happen as they are so decorative, it will develop seeds in the neck as well as within the base, and dry out.

three-cheese cauliflower gratinato

Reminiscent of the best homemade mac-and-cheese, only lighter, you'd be hard put to find a more popular side dish for roast meat or turkey. With its crisp golden topping and creamy-chunky interior, it also makes a satisfying supper dish on its own.

SERVES 6 AS A SIDE DISH, 2 OR 3 AS A MAIN COURSE

Preheat the oven to 375°F. Lightly butter a 6-cup shallow baking dish.

Cook the cauliflower in boiling, salted water until tender, about 10 minutes. Drain, transfer to a large bowl, and add 3 tablespoons of the butter. Mash coarsely with a pastry cutter or potato masher. Stir in the Fontina, pecorino, and Parmesan. Set aside.

BÈCHAMEL SAUCE: Melt the butter in a saucepan over low heat. Add the rice flour and potato starch and cook for 1 minute, stirring constantly. Add the hot milk in a slow stream, whisking at the same time. Increase the heat to medium and bring to a boil. Reduce heat to low and simmer for 5 minutes, stirring frequently. Season to taste with salt, pepper, and nutmeg. (Don't overdo the nutmeg; a little is good, too much is overpowering.)

Stir ½ cup of the bèchamel sauce into the cauliflower mixture. Taste for seasoning. Spoon the cauliflower mixture into the baking dish and cover with the remaining sauce. Sprinkle with the bread crumbs and dot with the remaining tablespoon of butter. Grate a little additional Parmesan on top.

Bake until bubbling and the surface is golden brown, about 25 minutes. Let cool for 10 minutes before serving.

4 tablespoons unsalted butter, plus extra for baking dish

1 cauliflower (about 2½ pounds), cored and cut into florets

Fine sea salt

2 ounces (about ½ cup) Fontina or Gruyère, cut in small dice

2 ounces (about ½ cup) grated Pecorino Romano

1 ounce (about ¼ cup) grated Parmigiano-Reggiano, plus extra for topping

BÈCHAMEL SAUCE (SALSA BESCIAMELLA)

2 tablespoons unsalted butter

1 tablespoon white rice flour

1 tablespoon potato starch

1½ cups whole or part skim milk, heated

Fine sea salt and freshly ground white pepper

Small pinch grated nutmeg

¼ cup Homemade Bread Crumbs (page 163)

sliced brussels sprouts
with crispy crumbs

*Forget the overcooked, watery Brussels sprouts of horrid memory. "Little cabbages,"
or cavolini du bruxelles, take on a new and delightful character when briefly sautéed,
Italian style. Serve to accompany roasted or sautéed pork or as a warm appetizer.*

SERVES 4 AS AN APPETIZER OR SIDE DISH

**½ pound
Brussels sprouts**

**2 tablespoons
extra-virgin olive oil**

**¾ cup tiny red
grape tomatoes**

3 tablespoons water

**1 tablespoon unsalted
butter**

**2 tablespoons
Homemade Bread
Crumbs (page 163) or
pine nuts**

**Fine sea salt and freshly
ground black pepper**

Trim the Brussels sprouts, cut in half, and slice very thinly parallel with the stalk.

Warm the olive oil in a large skillet over moderate heat. Add the sliced sprouts, and sauté, turning often, about 1 minute. Add the tomatoes and water, cover, and steam until tender, 2 or 3 minutes. The slices should remain intact and be tender-crisp, but if they are still too firm, continue sautéing for another minute.

Meanwhile, melt the butter in a small skillet over moderate heat. Stir in the bread crumbs and sauté until crisp and golden, about 30 seconds. (If using pine nuts, sauté in butter just until they start to brown, about 20 seconds.)

Season the sprouts and tomatoes with salt and pepper, divide among warmed plates, and sprinkle with the toasted crumbs or pine nuts.

baked celery with parmesan

Celery doesn't usually engender much enthusiasm, but when cooked this way it undergoes a Cinderella-like transformation and wins surprised approval.

SERVES 4 AS AN APPETIZER OR SIDE DISH

Cut a slice off the base of each celery bunch and separate into stalks, reserving the tougher outer ones for another use.

Using a vegetable peeler, zip any tough strings off the backs of all the bigger stalks. Trim the celery into ½-inch x 2-inch batons, and be sure to include the tender, leafy centers.

Bring the chicken broth to a boil and add the celery. Reduce the heat to low and simmer until just tender, about 20 minutes. Drain well, reserving what's left of the broth for another use.

Meanwhile, preheat the oven to 425°F. Grease an 8 x 10 x 2-inch baking dish with 1 tablespoon of the butter.

Crush the anise seeds lightly using a mortar and pestle (or the back of a small saucepan) to release the flavor, and sprinkle them in the baking dish. Add the drained celery, stacking it in neat rows, which makes it easier to serve. Drizzle with the cream. Season with a little salt and a generous grinding of pepper.

Combine the cheese and bread crumbs, and sprinkle on top. Dot with the remaining tablespoon of the butter.

Bake until golden, about 15 minutes.

2 bunches celery,
to yield about 1 pound
inner stalks

2 cups gluten-free
chicken broth

2 tablespoons unsalted
butter

¼ teaspoon anise or
fennel seeds

2 tablespoons heavy
cream or milk

Fine sea salt and freshly
grated black pepper

1 ounce (about ¼ cup)
grated Parmigiano-
Reggiano or Grana
Padana

¼ cup Homemade Bread
Crumbs (page 163)

stuffed chard bundles

Eating your leafy greens was never more inviting. These roll-ups are wonderful served as an antipasto or main course. Choose large chard leaves for this dish.

SERVES 6 AS AN APPETIZER, 2 OR 3 AS A MAIN COURSE

1 large bunch red chard, about 1 pound, rinsed

3 tablespoons extra-virgin olive oil

3 tablespoons chopped pancetta or unsmoked bacon (salt pork)

2 garlic cloves, chopped

3 tablespoons dried currants

3 tablespoons roughly chopped walnuts

3 tablespoons capers, rinsed and drained

Fine sea salt and freshly ground black pepper

¾ cup Homemade Bread Crumbs (page 163)

3 ounces (about ¾ cup) grated Parmigiano-Reggiano

Olive oil spray

Preheat the oven to 375°F. Cut the red stems and central ribs out of the chard leaves. Chop enough of the stems and ribs to make 1 cup.

Bring a large pan of water to a rolling boil, add the chard leaf halves, and blanch for 30 seconds, or just long enough to wilt them. Holding the leaves back with a wooden spoon, drain the pan and add cold water to stop the cooking. Drain again, and carefully lay the leaves out flat on a work surface.

Warm 1 tablespoon of the olive oil in a skillet over moderate heat. Add the pancetta and cook until the fat starts to melt, about 1 minute. Add the chopped chard ribs, garlic, currants, walnuts, and capers, and let cook, stirring, until the chard mixture softens slightly, about 2 minutes. Remove from the heat. Add a little salt (the pancetta and cheese are salty, so add sparingly), and a generous grinding of black pepper. Stir in ½ cup of the bread crumbs and ½ cup of the cheese.

Pour the remaining 2 tablespoons of olive oil into a 10 x 14-inch shallow baking dish. Set out 12 chard leaf halves, overlapping as needed (the greens will stick together) to make ovals about 6 x 4 inches. Top each green oval with about 2 tablespoons of the stuffing, placing it on the bottom third. Roll up like a jelly roll, tucking in the sides as best you can.

Transfer the roll-ups to the baking dish, seam side down, turning them once in the oil. The ends can touch (especially if the filling shows), but leave a little room for expansion on the long sides.

Top the roll-ups with the remaining ¼ cup of bread crumbs and ¼ cup of cheese and spray with olive oil. Cover the dish with aluminum foil and bake for 25 minutes. Uncover and bake for a further 10 minutes, to brown and crisp the top. Serve warm or at room temperature.

sautéed chard with balsamic vinegar and croutons

A popular first course, the sweet-and-sour character of chard served with balsamic vinegar and currants makes it particularly appealing. Italian cooks like to serve this and many other dark green leafy vegetables at room temperature. When cooked this way, chard is good hot, warm, or cold.

SERVES 4 AS AN APPETIZER

Cut the stems and central ribs out of the chard leaves, and chop them into small dice. Chop the leaves coarsely.

Warm 3 tablespoons of the olive oil in a large skillet over moderate heat. Add the bread cubes and fry until golden, turning often, about 2 minutes. Season with salt and pepper and set the pan aside.

Warm the remaining 3 tablespoons of olive oil in a large sauté pan over moderate heat. Add the onion, garlic, and chopped stems and sauté until tender but not colored, about 7 minutes. Add the chopped chard leaves, currants, and water. Bring to a boil. Cover, reduce the heat slightly, and steam until tender, about 5 minutes more.

Season the chard with salt and pepper and stir in the vinegar. Divide among four heated plates and sprinkle each serving with one-quarter of the crispy croutons.

VARIATION: You can cook broccoli rabe (*rapini*) in exactly the same way, but chop the tough stems off at leaf level and discard them. Then blanch the leaves and florets in salted boiling water for 3 minutes, drain, squeeze dry, and sauté. When cooked this way, even the skeptical take to rapini's characteristic, slightly bitter flavor.

1 medium bunch red or rainbow chard, about ³/₄ pound, rinsed

6 tablespoons extra-virgin olive oil

1¹/₂ cups slightly stale, ³/₄-inch gluten-free bread cubes (page 163)

Fine sea salt and freshly ground black pepper

1 small onion, finely chopped

2 garlic cloves, thinly sliced

2 tablespoons dried currants

¹/₄ cup water

1 tablespoon balsamic vinegar

spinach and potato fritatta

Simple to make (frozen spinach saves a lot of time, but you can substitute blanched and squeezed fresh spinach if you like) and extremely versatile, this crustless vegetarian tart makes a wonderful snack. As it travels well, it also makes great picnic and potluck fare. The fritatta will keep refrigerated for three days, should it manage to escape attention for that long.

SERVES 8 AS AN APPETIZER, 4 AS A LIGHT MAIN COURSE

1 large Yukon Gold or other waxy potato, about 6 ounces

2 tablespoons extra-virgin olive oil, plus extra for greasing dish

3 large green onions, most of the stems included, finely sliced

8 ounces loose-pack frozen spinach

4 large eggs

3 ounces (about ½ cup) fresh white goat cheese, crumbled

2 tablespoons heavy cream

2 ounces (about ½ cup) grated Pecorino Romano

Fine sea salt and freshly ground black pepper

Pinch nutmeg

Preheat the oven to 375°F. Grease an 8 x 10 x 2-inch shallow baking dish lightly with olive oil.

Peel the potato and slice ½-inch thick. Drop into boiling, salted water, return to a boil, and cook until barely tender, about 5 minutes. Drain and cut into small cubes.

Warm the olive oil in a large skillet over moderate heat. Sauté the green onions until lightly softened, about 30 seconds. Add the frozen spinach and cook until thawed, stirring often, about 2 minutes (if using blanched fresh spinach, cook for 1 minute). Let cool slightly.

Beat the eggs in a bowl. Stir in the goat cheese, cream, all but 2 tablespoons of the pecorino, spinach, and diced potato. Season with a little salt, a generous grinding of pepper, and the nutmeg. Spoon into the baking dish, smooth the top, and sprinkle with the remaining 2 tablespoons of pecorino.

Bake until risen and dappled golden brown, about 30 minutes. Serve warm, not blistering hot, or at room temperature.

sautéed spinach
with garlic and currants

Flavorful fresh spinach with shield-shaped leaves is called for here, not the miniature round-leafed variety that comes packed in bags for salad.

SERVES 4 AS AN APPETIZER

Warm 3 tablespoons of the olive oil in a large skillet over moderate heat. Add the bread cubes and fry until golden, turning often, about 2 minutes. Season with salt and pepper, and set the pan aside.

Warm the remaining 2 tablespoons of olive oil in a large sauté pan over moderate heat. Add the onion and garlic and sauté until softened but not colored, about 5 minutes. Stir in the spinach, currants, and water. Stir to mix. Cover, reduce the heat slightly, and steam until tender, about 5 minutes. Season with salt and pepper, and stir in the vinegar. Divide among warmed plates and sprinkle each serving with one-quarter of the croutons.

TIP: To prepare fresh spinach, nip off the stems and drop the leaves in a large bowl of water. Lift them out (any sand will sink to the bottom), and repeat the process with fresh water until the water is clear. Drain but don't dry the leaves.

5 tablespoons
extra-virgin olive oil

1½ cups day-old, ¾-inch
gluten-free bread cubes
(page 163)

Fine sea salt and freshly
ground black pepper

1 small onion,
finely chopped

2 garlic cloves,
thinly sliced

1 large bunch spinach,
about 1 pound, stemmed,
rinsed, and roughly
chopped

2 tablespoons dried
currants

2 tablespoons water

1 tablespoon
red wine vinegar

creamy stuffed eggplant with tomato and olives

One of the best comfort foods imaginable, the creamy-chewy filling for these baked eggplants has sweet and savory accents and contrasts perfectly with the crispy topping. The tender (and nutritious) eggplant shells can be eaten or not, as you please.

SERVES 4 AS A MAIN COURSE

2 purple globe eggplants, long rather than round, about 12 ounces each

3 tablespoons extra-virgin olive oil

1 medium onion, finely chopped

½ cup raw long-grain white rice

½ teaspoon dried thyme

Fine sea salt and freshly ground black pepper

1 cup gluten-free vegetable broth

4 tablespoons dried currants

4 tablespoons pine nuts

2 ounces (about ½ cup) grated Parmigiano-Reggiano

2 medium vine-ripened tomatoes, peeled and chopped

10 Kalamata olives, pitted and sliced

½ cup chopped parsley, plus 2 tablespoons

½ cup Homemade Bread Crumbs (page 163)

Olive oil spray

Slice the eggplants in half lengthways, retaining the leafy cap. Scoop out the flesh, leaving a ¼-inch thick shell, and chop finely. Oil a shallow baking dish just large enough to hold the four eggplant shells with 1 tablespoon of the olive oil, and arrange them in it "nose to tail," hollow side up.

Warm 2 tablespoons of the olive oil in a large skillet over moderate heat. Add the onion and sauté until softened, about 5 minutes. Add the rice and stir well. Stir in the chopped eggplant and thyme, season with salt and pepper, and sauté until the eggplant starts to turn glassy-looking, about 5 minutes.

Add the broth and bring to a boil. Cover the pan, reduce the heat to low, and simmer until the rice is almost tender, about 15 minutes.

Meanwhile, preheat the oven to 375°F. Add the currants, pine nuts, ¼ cup of the cheese, and the tomato, olives, and ½ cup parsley to the pan containing the rice, and stir to combine.

Spoon the stuffing mixture into the eggplant shells. Combine the remaining ¼ cup of cheese with the bread crumbs and sprinkle on top. Spray the stuffed eggplants with olive oil.

Bake until the stuffing is tender and the topping is golden brown (lay a sheet of aluminum foil over the eggplant if the tops start to brown too quickly), about 45 minutes. Let cool for 10 minutes before serving. Sprinkle with the remaining 2 tablespoons of parsley.

EGGPLANT:
TO SALT OR NOT TO SALT?

EGGPLANTS GOT THEIR odd name because the small round white ones do in fact look like eggs, but the resemblance ends there.

The interior of large globe eggplants, whatever their color—white, lavender, purple, or striped—is usually creamy and feels quite firm but is actually multicellular and spongelike. A large, older eggplant develops brown seeds that contain a bitter liquid, and salting draws some of it out, so for a mature vegetable it's a good idea.

To salt an eggplant, slice it into 1/2-inch thick rounds and season the slices generously with coarse sea salt or kosher salt. Let the slices drain for 30 minutes; rinse well and pat dry. Be careful not to oversalt when cooking.

Conversely, firm young globe eggplants and long, slender Japanese eggplants have few seeds and are not bitter, so salting them is unnecessary.

grilled eggplant stacks
with goat cheese

This attractive but simple appetizer can be made very successfully using a square, ridged, stove-top grill pan, which holds eight slices of eggplant nicely. Of course, if you have an outdoor grill all fired up and ready to go, so much the better. In that case, you can multiply the recipe ad infinitum.

SERVES 4 AS AN APPETIZER

1 purple globe eggplant (choose a rather elongated one, about ³/₄ pound), unpeeled, ends trimmed off, sliced ³/₄-inch thick

2 large vine-ripened tomatoes (about the same diameter as the eggplant), sliced ³/₄-inch thick

1 egg yolk

Fine sea salt and freshly ground black pepper

¹/₄ cup white rice flour

Olive oil spray

1 tablespoon extra-virgin olive oil

2 ounces fresh white goat cheese, cut into 4 slices

1 tablespoon shredded basil

Set out eight "center cut" eggplant slices and four "center cut" tomato slices and reserve the remainder for another use.

Beat the egg yolk in a shallow bowl and add the tomato slices, turning to coat. Season with salt and pepper. Have the rice flour ready on a small plate alongside.

Warm a ridged grill pan over moderate heat until hot: a few drops of water flicked onto the surface should bounce and hiss. Spray the eggplant slices with olive oil, and place in the pan, oiled side down. Cook until the undersides are browned, about 6 minutes. Spray again with olive oil, turn over, and cook the second side until browned, 3 minutes more. Season lightly with salt and pepper.

Meanwhile, heat the olive oil in a skillet. Dip the tomato slices in the flour to coat, shaking off any excess, and fry on both sides until golden brown, about 4 minutes total.

For each serving, stack up a slice of eggplant, a slice of tomato, and a slice of goat cheese. Top with a second slice of eggplant and a scattering of basil.

soup for supper

"MINESTRONE" IS A CATCH-ALL name for soup (minestra: soup; minestrone: the big soup). Italian cooks thicken satisfying, economical minestrone with pasta, potatoes, rice, or beans and sometimes use a combination of all four. You'll find many delightful variations below, as well as some other essential bean- and vegetable-based recipes. Even if you're not making gluten-free soup for a hungry horde, cook a big batch anyway and refrigerate or freeze the balance for another day. Finding homemade soup in the freezer is like discovering gold, and a big bowlful makes a comforting meal on a cold night. (Be sure to set aside the amount you plan to save before adding rice or gluten-free pasta or rice, as neither one chills satisfactorily.)

Rich with veggies and beans and ladled over toasted gluten-free bread and crispy pancetta, this thick soup makes a warming, filling, one-dish meal.

SERVES 4 TO 6

Separate the chard leaves and stems. Stack, roll, and slice the leaves thinly. Chop the stems finely.

Sauté the pancetta in a heavy pot over moderate heat until it starts to brown, about 2 minutes. Remove and reserve.

Add the olive oil to the pan and heat. Stir in the onion, celery, and chopped chard stems and sauté until softened but not colored, about 8 minutes. Add the broth, Marinara Sauce, water, rice, and beans and bring to a boil. Reduce the heat and simmer, partially covered, for 10 minutes.

Add the chard leaves to the pot and continue simmering until the rice is tender, another 10 minutes. The soup should be thick, but add a little more water if needed. Season to taste with salt and pepper.

Preheat a ridged grill pan or skillet. Spray both sides of the bread slices with olive oil and grill or fry until lightly browned, turning once.

Divide the toasted bread among soup bowls, and top with the reserved pancetta. Ladle the soup on top, and sprinkle with the Parmesan.

1 small bunch chard, about 8 ounces, rinsed and drained

2 ounces chopped pancetta or unsmoked bacon (salt pork)

2 tablespoons extra-virgin olive oil

1 small onion, chopped

2 celery ribs, de-stringed and finely chopped

2 cups gluten-free beef, chicken, or vegetable broth

1 cup Marinara Sauce (page 44), or from a jar

2 cups water

⅓ cup long-grain white rice

1 (15-ounce) can white kidney beans (cannellini), rinsed and drained, or 2 cups homemade beans

Fine sea salt and freshly ground black pepper

8 to 12 slices Italian-Style Baguette (page 158), ½-inch thick

Olive oil spray

4 to 6 tablespoons freshly grated Parmigiano-Reggiano, or more to taste

---

DE-STRINGING CELERY

WHEN PREPARING CELERY, take the strings off the back of the outer ribs with a vegetable peeler before chopping. These fibers are extremely tough and don't soften completely during cooking. Incidentally, the tender leaves at the center of a bunch of celery have concentrated nutrients, so always use them.

marinara sauce

¼ cup extra-virgin olive oil

2 large garlic cloves, slightly crushed

1 (28-ounce) can Italian plum tomatoes, juice included

Fine sea salt and freshly ground black pepper

1 tablespoon shredded basil or flat-leaf parsley

Warm the olive oil in a heavy saucepan over moderate heat. Add the garlic and cook until golden, about 5 minutes. Discard the garlic, and stir in the tomatoes. Crush with a wooden spoon or potato masher. Season lightly with salt and pepper. Bring to a boil, reduce the heat slightly, and cook until somewhat thickened, stirring occasionally, about 20 minutes. Remove from the heat and stir in the basil. Taste for seasoning.

dried beans

A godsend for the gluten-challenged cook, plain canned beans offer convenience as well as great nutrition, but cooking them yourself makes economic sense if you're cooking for lots of people.

Italian cooks favor large white cannellini beans for minestrone and various other dishes (see Tuna Salad with White Beans on page 129 or Penne and Beans with Pork Ragù on page 69), but feel free to use Great Northern or small white (navy) beans instead.

Always use freshly packaged beans; if they've been on a shelf for a long time, they'll remain obstinately hard no matter how long you cook them. All varieties—white, red, pink, and speckled—need to be presoaked before cooking. You can soak them overnight in cold water, or use the short-cut boiling water method outlined below. Lentils are an exception in the world of dried legumes; they don't need soaking and cook in about 35 minutes.

You'll need a 4-quart pot to cook 1 pound of dried beans, which will swell to roughly four times their original size. Naturally, the recipe can be doubled.

MAKES APPROXIMATELY 8 CUPS

Bring the water to a rolling boil over high heat.

Rinse the beans in a bowl of cold water and discard any little stones or other debris. Drain the beans and add them to the boiling water. Return to a boil for 2 minutes. Remove the pot from the heat and let the beans soak for 1 hour.

When the hour is up, add the salt (it doesn't make beans hard if added at the start of cooking—that's a myth—and gives them a much deeper flavor) and bring to a simmer. Skim off any frothy scum that may float to the surface. Simmer gently, uncovered, until the beans are just tender, about 1 hour for small beans, 1½ hours for Great Northern. Add more boiling water if necessary to keep the beans covered. Leave the beans in their cooking liquid until ready to use, then drain.

The cooked beans can be refrigerated for three days, or frozen. Two-cup containers, the approximate equivalent of a 15-ounce can, are usually the most practical.

3 quarts water

1 pound (about 2 cups) dried beans, such as cannellini, small white, or Great Northern

½ teaspoon fine sea salt

minestrone with rutabaga and beans

*Not as well known as they should be given their sweet flavor and good texture,
nutrient-dense, yellow-fleshed rutabagas make a delicious addition to minestrone.*

SERVES 4 TO 6

2 tablespoons extra-virgin olive oil

3 ounces diced pancetta or unsmoked bacon (salt pork)

1 onion, quartered and finely sliced

3 celery ribs, de-stringed and finely chopped

1 large rutabaga (yellow turnip), finely chopped

1 teaspoon chopped rosemary

1 (28-ounce) can Italian plum tomatoes, juice included

2 garlic cloves, finely chopped

4 cups gluten-free chicken broth

1 (15-ounce) can white kidney beans (cannellini), rinsed and drained, or 2 cups cooked white beans

Fine sea salt and freshly ground black pepper

½ cup (2 ounces) gluten-free pasta elbows

4 tablespoons chopped flat-leaf parsley

4 tablespoons freshly grated Parmigiano-Reggiano, or more to taste

Warm the olive oil in a large pot over moderate heat. Add the pancetta, onion, celery, rutabaga, and rosemary and sauté, stirring frequently, until slightly softened, about 5 minutes.

Add the tomatoes, garlic, chicken broth, and beans and season lightly with salt and pepper. Crush the tomatoes with a wooden spoon.

Bring to a boil, reduce the heat to low, and simmer, partially covered, until the fresh vegetables are tender, about 25 minutes.

Meanwhile, cook the pasta in boiling, salted water until tender, about 10 minutes. Taste test often as brands differ. (Cooking gluten-free pasta separately gives more reliable results.)

Drain the pasta, reserving the water, and add the pasta to the soup. Stir in the parsley. Minestrone is meant to be thick, but if there's not enough liquid, add a little of the hot pasta water. Taste and adjust seasoning as needed. Serve sprinkled with the Parmesan.

minestrone with seafood and pasta

This thick and hearty soup makes inspired use of frozen seafood. Alternatively, you can substitute 1 pound of any frozen or fresh firm white fish, such as halibut or cod, cut into 1-inch cubes, which will cook in 2 minutes or less.

SERVES 4 TO 6

Warm 2 tablespoons of the olive oil in a large saucepan over moderate heat. Add the onion, carrot, and celery and sauté until softened but not colored, about 5 minutes.

Add the garlic, tomatoes, and zucchini and simmer for 10 minutes.

Crumble the saffron over the vegetables and stir in the fennel seeds. Stir in the clam juice and water. Season with 1 teaspoon of salt and a generous grinding of black pepper. Bring to a boil, then reduce the heat to low and simmer until the vegetables are tender, about 20 minutes.

Meanwhile, cook the pasta in boiling, salted water until tender, about 8 minutes. Taste test often as brands differ. Drain the pasta, reserving some of the water, and toss with the remaining tablespoon of olive oil to prevent sticking.

Add the frozen seafood to the soup and simmer until it is tender and opaque, 1 to 2 minutes. Stir in the pasta, and add a little pasta water if necessary. Taste for seasoning. Divide the soup among bowls and sprinkle with the parsley.

Ingredients

- 3 tablespoons extra-virgin olive oil
- 1 medium onion, finely chopped
- 1 medium carrot, finely chopped
- 2 celery ribs, de-stringed and finely chopped
- 2 garlic cloves, chopped
- 2 cups peeled and chopped ripe fresh or canned tomatoes
- 2 medium zucchini, diced
- Pinch saffron threads
- ½ teaspoon fennel seeds
- 1 (8-ounce) bottle clam juice plus 2 cups water, or 3 cups water
- Fine sea salt and freshly ground black pepper
- 6 ounces gluten-free spaghetti, broken into short lengths (about 1½ cups)
- 1 pound frozen peeled shrimp, bay scallops, or calamari, or a mix of all three
- 4 tablespoons chopped flat-leaf parsley

GLUTEN-FREE PASTA ALERT

IT'S BEST TO cook gluten-free pasta intended for soup separately, so that it doesn't get overcooked. Toss with a little olive oil and add just before serving. Also, if you plan to reheat minestrone, any pasta left in the soup would absorb too much liquid and disintegrate, so cooking it separately is more practical.

Remember that boiling-hot pasta cooking water has value as it picks up both starch and flavors. It's much better than plain water for smoothing out a too-thick sauce or soup, as it also contributes texture and a touch more flavor.

minestrone with pesto, genoese style

The Italian province of Liguria lies between Tuscany and Provence, with a narrow coastal strip that faces the northern Mediterranean. The once mighty port of Genoa is the home of pesto, a basil and garlic-scented sauce that appeals to most people the way catnip attracts cats. Sensational on pasta, it does equally great things for minestrone. This recipe makes about 6 cups of hearty soup.

SERVES 4 TO 6

4 tablespoons extra-virgin olive oil

1 yellow onion, chopped

1 medium carrot, finely diced

2 small celery ribs, de-stringed and finely diced

1 large baking potato, such as Russet or Idaho, peeled and diced

1 (15-ounce) can white kidney beans (cannellini), rinsed and drained, or 2 cups cooked white beans

1 (14- to 15-ounce) can diced Italian plum tomatoes, juice included

Fine sea salt and freshly ground black pepper

3 cups gluten-free vegetable broth

1 cup frozen peas

1 cup (4 ounces) small, gluten-free pasta shells

½ cup Pesto Sauce (page 49), or from a jar

2 ounces (about ½ cup) grated Pecorino Romano

Warm 2 tablespoons of the olive oil in a large pot over moderate heat. Add the onion, carrot, and celery. Sauté until slightly softened, about 7 minutes. Add the potato, beans, and tomatoes. Season with salt and pepper, add the vegetable broth, and bring to a boil.

Reduce the heat to low, and simmer, partly covered, until all the vegetables are tender but not mushy, about 30 minutes. Stir in the peas, and simmer for 2 minutes more.

Meanwhile, boil the pasta in salted water until al dente, about 10 minutes. Taste test often, as brands differ. Remove with a slotted spoon, and add to the soup, which will be very thick. Add just enough of the pasta water to thin it down a little, according to preference. Stir in the remaining 2 tablespoons of olive oil, and taste for seasoning.

Ladle the soup into shallow bowls. Pass the pesto for diners to stir into the soup themselves (1 tablespoon per serving is about right). Pass the pecorino for sprinkling on top.

pesto sauce

MAKES APPROXIMATELY ½ CUP

In a food processor, combine the garlic, basil leaves, pine nuts, and 1 tablespoon of the olive oil. Process in short bursts, scraping down the bowl occasionally and adding the remaining 3 tablespoons of olive oil 1 tablespoon at a time, until the sauce is slightly chunky. Don't overblend. Stir in the Parmesan, and add salt to taste. Transfer to a glass bowl, and cover with a thin film of olive oil until ready to serve. If storing in the freezer, omit the cheese and add it later, when thawed.

1 garlic clove, roughly chopped

1½ cups tightly packed small basil leaves, rinsed and thoroughly dried

4 tablespoons raw pine nuts

4 tablespoons extra-virgin olive oil

1 ounce (about ¼ cup) freshly grated Parmigiano-Reggiano

Fine sea salt

off-the-shelf white bean, sage, and pumpkin soup

This creamy soup is quickly made, satisfying, affordable, and healthful. What more could one ask?

SERVES 2 TO 3

1 cup (2 ounces) gluten-free pasta spirals

2 tablespoons extra-virgin olive oil

1 small onion, finely sliced (or ⅓ cup frozen chopped onions)

1 garlic clove, chopped

1 teaspoon crumbled dried sage, or more to taste

3 cups gluten-free chicken broth or vegetable broth

1 (15-ounce) can unsweetened pumpkin purée

1 (15-ounce) can white kidney beans (cannellini), rinsed and drained

Fine sea salt and freshly ground black pepper

1 teaspoon red wine vinegar, optional

2 tablespoons chopped flat-leaf parsley, optional

Freshly grated Parmigiano-Reggiano

Bring a pot of salted water to a boil. Stir in the pasta. Cook until al dente, about 8 minutes. Taste test often as brands differ. Drain, toss with 1 tablespoon of the olive oil, and set aside.

Meanwhile, heat the remaining tablespoon of olive oil in a saucepan. Add the onion, garlic, and sage and cook over low heat until softened, about 3 minutes. Add the broth and bring to a simmer.

Stir in the pumpkin purée and kidney beans. Bring to a boil, then reduce the heat to low and simmer for about 5 minutes, to blend the flavors. Season to taste with salt and pepper and add the vinegar, if using.

Stir in the pasta. Divide the soup among shallow soup bowls. Top with the optional parsley and Parmesan to taste.

lentil, rice, and spinach soup

Umbria is famed for the quality and flavor of its lentils, which, unlike common brown lentils, don't become floury when cooked. If you can't find Umbrian lentils (available in Italian delis and some natural foods stores), use green le Puy lentils from France instead, which have similar characteristics and are more readily available. Unlike other high-protein dried legumes, lentils don't need to be soaked before you cook them.

SERVES 4

heavy saucepan over moderate heat, add the onion and carrot, and sauté until the onion turns pale gold, about 5 minutes. Add the garlic and pancetta, if using, and sauté for 1 minute.

Stir in the tomatoes, breaking them up with a wooden spoon. Add the lentils, salt and pepper, and the broth and water mixture. Bring the soup to a boil, reduce the heat to low, and cook until the lentils are tender, 35 to 40 minutes.

Stir in the spinach, and cook until thawed, about 2 minutes. Add the rice and cook until heated through, another 2 minutes. The soup should be very thick, so add a little water if needed. Taste for seasoning.

Divide the soup among four wide soup bowls and top with the Parmesan.

2 tablespoons extra-virgin olive oil

1 small onion, finely chopped

1 carrot, finely chopped

2 garlic cloves, finely chopped

2 tablespoons finely chopped pancetta or unsmoked bacon (salt pork), optional

1 (14- to 15-ounce) can Italian plum tomatoes to supply 1 cup tomatoes, juice included (reserve remainder for another use)

1 cup Umbrian brown lentils or green le Puy lentils, rinsed

Fine sea salt and freshly ground black pepper

3 cups gluten-free chicken or vegetable broth mixed with 2 cups water

4 to 6 ounces frozen loose-pack spinach (about 1½ cups)

1 cup cooked brown rice or quinoa

4 tablespoons Parmigiano-Reggiano

Warm the olive oil in a

cioppino

A San Francisco original, cioppino (chuh-pea-no) originated in the 1930s, when immigrant Italian fisherman all contributed a little something from the day's catch to a communal stew kettle on the wharf. No one really knows, but the name might be an Italian-American version of "chip in." You can use any combination of fish and seafood you like; just be sure to serve cioppino with crusty, gluten-free bread for dunking, a bottle of wine, and plenty of paper napkins as it's gloriously messy. Sensational for a casual party—the recipe can be multiplied ad infinitum—the tomato base can be made ahead. The seafood medley, which can vary according to what's available, takes just a few minutes to cook.

S ERVES 4 TO 6

TOMATO BASE

¼ cup extra-virgin olive oil

2 medium yellow onions, chopped

2 garlic cloves, sliced

Pinch hot red pepper flakes

½ teaspoon fennel seeds

1 teaspoon dried oregano

4 cups peeled and chopped vine-ripened tomatoes, or 1 (32-ounce) can diced Italian plum tomatoes, juice included

2 tablespoons red wine vinegar

2 (8-ounce) bottles clam juice (or 1 bottle clam juice and 1 cup water)

2 bay leaves

1 cup dry white or red wine, according to preference or what's on hand

Fine sea salt and freshly ground black pepper

TOMATO BASE: Combine the olive oil, onions, garlic, hot pepper flakes, fennel seeds, and oregano in a large, heavy pot. Warm gently over medium-low heat, stirring, until the onion is softened but not colored and the mixture is aromatic, about 3 minutes.

Stir in the tomatoes, vinegar, clam juice, bay leaves, and wine. Bring to a boil, reduce the heat to low, cover and simmer until well amalgamated, about 45 minutes. Keep checking the consistency and add a little water if the mixture thickens too much. Season with salt and pepper.

Fish and Seafood: Scrub the mussels under cold running water and set aside. Cut the fish into 1-inch chunks. Combine the shrimp, scallops, and calamari in a bowl.

Bring the tomato base to a simmer. Add the mussels and fish, cover the pot and cook until the shells open, about 2 minutes.

Stir in the shrimp, scallops, and calamari and simmer uncovered until opaque and just cooked through, about 2 minutes more. (Do not overcook, the seafood will continue cooking after the pot is removed from the heat.)

Divide the cioppino among large soup bowls, discarding the bay leaves. Serve with the baguette for dunking and put out bowls for the shells.

FISH AND SEAFOOD

24 mussels or clams, in the shell

1 pound white fish (bass, halibut, cod, or other firm variety)

24 large shrimp, peeled and deveined, tails left on

½ pound bay scallops

½ pound sliced calamari

2 Italian-Style Baguettes (page 158), thickly sliced

potato and zucchini soup
with mint and croutons

This fragrant soup can be made ahead and reheated before adding the cream and mint. Mint might seem like an unusual ingredient in the Italian kitchen, but it does get used now and then and adds bright flavor to what might otherwise be a pleasant but unexceptional soup. Don't bother with dried mint; it must be fresh.

SERVES 4 AS A FIRST COURSE

1 large leek, white and pale green part only

4 tablespoons unsalted butter

1 small floury baking potato, such as Russet or Idaho, about 6 ounces, peeled and diced

2 medium zucchini, unpeeled, diced

2 cups gluten-free chicken or vegetable broth, plus extra if needed

Fine sea salt and freshly ground white pepper

16 to 20 gluten-free bread cubes (page 163)

4 tablespoons heavy cream

1 tablespoon finely shredded fresh mint

Cut the leek in half lengthways, slice thinly, and submerge in a bowl of cold water. Lift from the water into a strainer (any sand will drop to the bottom of the bowl), and drain. Repeat if necessary.

Melt 2 tablespoons of the butter in a saucepan over low heat. Add the sliced leek and cook gently, partially covered, until softened but not colored, about 10 minutes. Stir in the potatoes and zucchini. Add the chicken broth, bring to a boil, and season the mixture with salt and a generous grinding of white pepper. Reduce the heat to low, and simmer until the vegetables are tender, about 15 minutes.

While the soup simmers, heat the remaining 2 tablespoons of butter in a skillet over moderate heat. Add the bread cubes and fry until golden, turning often, about 5 minutes. Remove the pan from the heat and set aside.

Using a potato masher, crush most of the vegetables into the broth. If it seems too thick, add a little more chicken broth and heat through. Stir in the cream and mint and taste for seasoning. Divide the soup among four soup bowls and float the croutons on top.

pasta

ALMOST EVERY REGION of Italy lays claim to having invented pasta, a magically pleasing combination of flour, water, olive oil, and in the case of fresh pasta, egg. (In fact, pasta seems to have originated in China, if finds at 6,000-year-old archaeological digs are anything to go by.) No matter. Endlessly versatile, pasta remains one of the glories of Italian cuisine.

Happily for the gluten-intolerant, gluten-free dried pasta in various shapes can now be found in natural foods stores and online, and there's a recipe for tender fresh pasta on page 70. A delight with nothing more than butter and Parmesan, this dough also makes fabulous Gorgonzola-filled ravioli: see how on page 73.

When cooked al dente and combined with one of the sumptuous sauces that follow, gluten-free pasta dishes are every bit as mouthwatering and satisfying as you could wish for, and most are quick to prepare.

fettuccine with walnuts, basil, and cream

When fresh basil is in season, prepare this speedy but elegant sauce for pasta.
It's like creamy Pasta Alfredo, with the addition of toasted nuts and aromatic fresh
basil. Simmering a clove of garlic in the pasta water lends a subtle touch.

SERVES 4 AS A FIRST COURSE

Preheat the oven to 350°F. Spread the walnuts on a baking sheet and toast until lightly browned and fragrant, about 8 minutes. Chop into small chunks.

Boil the fettuccine in salted water with the garlic until al dente, about 7 minutes. Brands differ, so taste test often. Drain the fettuccine and discard the garlic.

While the pasta cooks, stir the cream and butter together in a large skillet over low heat, until smooth and barely simmering. Add the fettuccine, walnuts, and salt and pepper to taste. Toss the pasta gently and divide among heated plates. Top with the shredded basil and Parmesan.

⅔ cup (4 ounces) walnut halves or pieces

10 to 12 ounces gluten-free fettuccine

1 large garlic clove, unpeeled, cut in half

¾ cup heavy cream

6 tablespoons unsalted butter

Fine sea salt and freshly ground black pepper

4 tablespoons shredded basil (shred just before using)

2 ounces (about ½ cup) grated Parmigiano-Reggiano

fettuccine with eggplant and peppers alla norma

Culinary legend has it that this simple but delectable dish was invented by an Italian chef to mark the first performance of Sicilian-born Vincenzo Bellini's grand opera, Norma, in 1831. Deep-frying the eggplant is traditional, but baking works well and is less caloric and far less work.

SERVES 4 AS A FIRST COURSE

1 medium globe eggplant, about ¾ pound, trimmed but not peeled

Olive oil spray

Fine sea salt and freshly ground black pepper

2 tablespoons extra-virgin olive oil

1 medium yellow onion, chopped

1 (14–15-ounce) can Italian plum tomatoes, drained (save the juice for another use)

2 garlic cloves, finely chopped

Pinch hot red pepper flakes

10 to 12 ounces gluten-free fettuccine

½ cup loosely packed basil leaves, chopped just before serving

Wedge of Pecorino Romano

Heat the oven to 400°F. Line a large, rimmed baking sheet with aluminum foil.

Slice the eggplant into ¾-inch thick slices and lay them on the baking sheet. Spray each one with olive oil. Turn them over and spray again. Bake until browned on the underside, about 15 minutes, then turn and bake for a further 10 minutes. Season lightly with salt and pepper.

Meanwhile, warm the olive oil in a skillet over moderate heat. Add the onion and sauté until softened, about 5 minutes. Quarter the tomatoes lengthways and then once across, to make large, even chunks, and add to the skillet. Stir in the garlic and hot pepper flakes and season with salt and pepper. Reduce the heat to low and simmer, partially covered, until the liquid has almost evaporated, about 15 minutes, stirring often. Quarter the eggplant slices and add to the sauce.

While the sauce cooks, boil the pasta in salted water, taste testing often, until al dente, about 7 minutes. Add to the sauce with the chopped basil, and toss gently. Divide the pasta among four heated shallow bowls. Garnish with curls of pecorino, shaving them off the wedge with a vegetable peeler.

fettuccine
with scallops and zucchini

Small, frozen bay scallops are at their best in this quick supper dish. Don't thaw them first, so their juices can mingle with the buttery wine and lemon sauce.

SERVES 2 AS A MAIN COURSE

Bring a large pot of salted water to a rolling boil, add the pasta, and cook, stirring occasionally, until al dente, about 7 minutes. Taste test often as brands differ.

Meanwhile, heat the olive oil and 1 tablespoon of the butter in a large skillet over moderate heat. Add the zucchini and garlic and cook until softened, about 2 minutes.

Separate the frozen scallops if any have stuck together and add them to the pan. Sauté for 2 minutes, then add the wine and simmer, stirring often, until the scallops are opaque and tender, about 2 minutes more. Season with salt and pepper. Grate the lemon zest finely over the scallops and add the capers.

Drain the pasta and add it to the skillet. Add the remaining 2 tablespoons butter, toss to mix, and divide between 2 heated plates.

TIP: It's best to follow the Italian lead here and don't add grated cheese; it rarely complements seafood.

6 to 8 ounces gluten-free fettuccine

1 tablespoon extra-virgin olive oil

3 tablespoons unsalted butter

2 small zucchini (4 ounces each), cut in 1/3-inch dice

1 garlic clove, chopped

3/4 pound frozen bay scallops, unthawed

1/4 cup dry white wine, such as Pinot Grigio

Fine sea salt and freshly ground black pepper

1 small lemon

2 teaspoons capers, rinsed and drained

fettuccine with olive oil, garlic, and parsley

A southern Italian standby, this combination of simple ingredients adds up to a quick, economical, and flavorful dish.

SERVES 4 AS A FIRST COURSE

10 to 12 ounces gluten-free fettuccine or spaghetti

½ cup extra-virgin olive oil

4 garlic cloves, halved

12 oil-cured black olives, pitted, and quartered

3 tablespoons chopped flat-leaf parsley

Cook the pasta in plenty of salted, boiling water until al dente, about 7 minutes. Taste test often as brands differ.

Meanwhile, warm the olive oil in a large skillet over medium-low heat. Add the garlic and simmer until it turns golden, about 2 minutes. Remove with a slotted spoon and discard. Add the olives and parsley, simmer for 1 minute, and remove from the heat.

Drain the pasta and add it to the skillet. Toss well. Serve without cheese.

PARSLEY: THE SUPER HERB

ASIDE FROM ADDING fresh flavor and color to pasta and countless other dishes, both flat-leaf and curly-leaf parsley are packed with valuable nutrients. (The flat-leaf variety has a more intense flavor, but either will do, and parsley's easy to grow if you have a garden.)

Just two tablespoons of chopped parsley provide over 150 percent of the recommended daily allowance of vitamin K; good amounts of Vitamin C, Vitamin A, folic acid, and iron; and it's rich in antioxidants. And all for 2.7 calories.

Storing parsley in the vegetable drawer of the refrigerator is not a good plan; it usually gets forgotten and turns slimy in revenge. Instead, support the stems in a tall glass of water the minute you get the bunch home from the store. If you change the water every day, it will keep for a week, and look decorative into the bargain. Alternatively, wash, dry, strip, and chop the leaves, and keep in a screw-topped glass jar in the freezer. The herbs won't freeze solid and can be spooned right from the jar. (You can do the same thing with chopped green onions.)

off-the-shelf fettuccine with pine nuts and peas

Simple but good, and a godsend if you're pressed for time or the refrigerator looks like Mother Hubbard's cupboard. This vegetarian recipe is, of course, easy to double.

SERVES 2 AS A MAIN COURSE

Bring a large pot of salted water to a rolling boil, add the pasta, and cook, stirring occasionally, until al dente, about 7 minutes. Taste test often as brands differ. Add the peas during the last 2 minutes of cooking time.

Meanwhile, heat the butter in a large skillet over moderate heat. As soon as it starts to turn a light golden brown, about 30 seconds, add the pine nuts and immediately remove from the heat. The nuts will continue to brown lightly. Season with salt and a generous grinding of black pepper.

Drain the pasta and peas and add them to the skillet with the butter and pine nuts. Toss to mix and divide the pasta between two heated plates. Top with the Parmesan.

TIP: Store pine nuts—in fact, all shelled nuts—in the freezer, as they can go rancid quite quickly otherwise. They will keep frozen for up to six months.

6 to 8 ounces gluten-free fettuccine or spaghetti

3/4 cup frozen peas

6 tablespoons unsalted butter, sliced

1/2 cup pine nuts

Fine sea salt and freshly ground black pepper

2 ounces (about 1/2 cup) grated Parmigiano-Reggiano, or more to taste

off-the-shelf tagliatelle with tuna

This Italian sauce for pasta puts canned tuna in a delicious and different setting. Glutino's gluten-free tagliatelle—relatively short, wide noodles—are first-rate, but if this type of pasta proves elusive, use fettuccine instead.

SERVES 2 AS A MAIN COURSE

6 to 8 ounces gluten-free tagliatelle

Fine sea salt and freshly ground black pepper

1 (6½-ounce) can oil-packed tuna, such as Genoa brand

4 tablespoons extra-virgin olive oil

3 canned Italian plum tomatoes, coarsely chopped

2 tablespoons chopped flat-leaf parsley, optional

2 tablespoons unsalted butter, sliced

Bring a large pot of salted water to a rolling boil, add the pasta, and cook, stirring occasionally, until al dente, about 5 minutes. Taste test often as brands differ.

Meanwhile, tip the tuna into a skillet and break into small bits with the side of a metal spoon. Add the olive oil and tomatoes and heat gently over low heat to just below a simmer. Turn off the heat and stir in the parsley, if using. Add the butter on top, which will gradually melt.

Drain the pasta and add it to the skillet. Toss to mix and divide the pasta between two heated plates. Serve without grated cheese.

CANNED TOMATOES

SWEET, JUICY, VINE-RIPENED heirloom tomatoes are only available for a few weeks each year (if at all, in some regions), so do as the Italians do and use best-quality canned tomatoes the rest of the time.

The best tomatoes for thick pasta sauces are undoubtedly those of San Marzano, a D.O.P (guaranteed origin) plum tomato of unrivalled sweetness and rich texture that grows in the volcanic soil below Mt. Vesuvius, near Naples. Containing very few seeds, they are so ripe and tender they can be crushed with a wooden spoon. See page 22 for more information on San Marzano tomatoes and domestic alternatives.

off-the-shelf spaghetti with pancetta and tomato

A little diced pancetta (unsmoked Italian bacon) adds inimitable flavor to countless Italian dishes and can be stored in the freezer for instant use. It is available in some markets already chopped in handy plastic pouches, or you can buy it thickly sliced and chop your own.

SERVES 2 AS A MAIN COURSE

Cook the pasta in boiling, salted water until al dente, about 7 minutes. Taste test often as brands differ.

Meanwhile, warm the olive oil in a sauté pan over moderate heat. Add the pancetta and cook until lightly colored, about 3 minutes. Add the garlic, tomatoes, oregano, and capers. Season lightly with salt and pepper.

Cook at a brisk simmer until slightly reduced, about 5 minutes. Taste for seasoning, add the drained pasta, and toss to mix. Divide the pasta between heated plates and top each serving with half the Parmesan.

TIP: For a vegetarian version of this recipe, substitute about 8 pitted and roughly chopped oil-cured or Kalamata olives for the pancetta and add a pinch of hot pepper flakes.

6 to 8 ounces gluten-free fettuccine or spaghetti

2 tablespoons extra-virgin olive oil

2 ounces chopped pancetta or unsmoked bacon (salt pork)

2 garlic cloves, chopped

1 (14–15-ounce) can chopped Italian plum tomatoes, juice included

½ teaspoon dried oregano

1 tablespoon rinsed and drained capers

Fine sea salt and freshly ground black pepper

4 tablespoons grated Parmigiano-Reggiano

spaghetti with caramelized red and yellow peppers

Oven-roasted bell peppers lend natural sweetness and color to this pasta dish and provide just the right flavor balance for pancetta and meaty, oil-cured black olives.

SERVES 4

2 medium-size red bell peppers, about 6 ounces each

2 yellow bell peppers, about 6 ounces each

3 tablespoons extra-virgin olive oil

1 medium yellow onion, halved and sliced

2 ounces chopped pancetta or unsmoked bacon (salt pork)

1 large garlic clove, chopped

½ cup black oil-cured olives, halved and pitted

Fine sea salt and freshly ground black pepper

10 to 12 ounces gluten-free spaghetti

Wedge of Parmigiano-Reggiano

2 tablespoons shredded basil or flat-leaf parsley

Preheat the oven to 425°F and line a rimmed baking sheet with aluminum foil.

Cut the peppers in half lengthways. Cut out the stems and ribs and discard any loose seeds. Arrange cut side down on the baking sheet. Bake until the skins look wrinkled and are starting to blacken in spots, about 25 minutes. Remove from the oven, cover with more foil, and let steam for 10 minutes. When the peppers are cool enough to handle, gently pull off the skins. Cut lengthways into wide strips.

Warm 2 tablespoons of the olive oil in a large sauté pan over moderate heat. Add the onion and pancetta. Sauté until the onion starts to turn transparent and the pancetta browns a little, about 5 minutes.

Add the garlic, reduce the heat slightly, and continue cooking until the onion is tender and pale gold, stirring often, about 5 minutes more. Add the olives and pepper strips. Season lightly with salt and generously with black pepper. Stir until heated through.

Meanwhile, cook the spaghetti in boiling, salted water until al dente, about 7 minutes. Taste test often as brands differ. Drain and toss with the remaining tablespoon of olive oil.

Divide the pasta among heated plates and top each serving with one quarter of the sauce. Garnish with curls of Parmesan, shaving them off the wedge with a vegetable peeler, and the shredded basil.

spirals with anchovies, olives, and mint

Fresh mint adds an unexpected grace note to this quick, easy, and appetizing pasta dish, which is especially suited to spirals as their nooks and crannies hold the sauce well. I like to let the mint, citrus zest, and fresh olive oil flavors predominate, but you can add grated Parmesan at the end if you wish.

SERVES 4

Bring a large pot of salted water to a boil, add the pasta, and cook until al dente, about 7 minutes. Taste test often as brands vary.

Meanwhile, warm ½ cup of the olive oil in a skillet over low heat. Add the garlic and cook until golden, about 2 minutes, and then discard. Add the anchovies and mash them with a wooden spoon to reduce them to a paste.

Remove from the heat and add the mint, capers, olives, and citrus zest. Add the 2 to 4 tablespoons of olive oil for fresh olive flavor.

Drain the pasta and add it to the skillet. Toss the pasta gently and divide it among four heated plates. Top with the chopped parsley.

Fine sea salt

10 to 12 ounces gluten-free spirals

½ to ¾ cup extra-virgin olive oil, plus 2 to 4 tablespoons

2 garlic cloves, cut in half

4 canned anchovy fillets, drained

6 mint leaves, chopped

4 teaspoons drained and rinsed, chopped if large, capers

16 Kalamata olives, pitted and finely chopped

1 teaspoon grated lemon or orange zest

2 tablespoons chopped flat-leaf parsley

spirals with turkey, sausage, and cream

Based on a classic creamy pasta sauce made with rabbit, a delicious white meat that's not readily available in the United States, ground turkey makes a satisfactory and inexpensive alternative.

SERVES 4

1 tablespoon extra-virgin olive oil

1 tablespoon unsalted butter

1 small yellow onion, finely chopped

8 ounces ground turkey thigh meat

1 mild Italian pork sausage (3 to 4 ounces), skin removed, chopped

Fine sea salt and freshly ground black pepper

¼ cup dry white wine

½ cup Marinara Sauce (page 44), or from a jar

½ cup gluten-free chicken broth, plus additional if needed

8 sage leaves, finely chopped, or ½ teaspoon dried sage

½ cup heavy cream

10 to 12 ounces gluten-free pasta spirals

2 tablespoons chopped flat-leaf parsley

4 tablespoons shredded Pecorino Romano, or more to taste

Warm the olive oil and butter in a large skillet over moderate heat. Add the onion and sauté until softened, about 3 minutes.

Crumble the ground turkey and sausage meat into the pan. Increase the heat and sauté, breaking up the mixture with a wooden spoon, until lightly browned, about 7 minutes. Season with salt and pepper.

Add the wine and let it evaporate by half. Stir in the Marinara Sauce, chicken broth, and sage, reduce the heat to low, and simmer, covered, until very tender, about 45 minutes, stirring occasionally and adding more broth if the sauce is becoming too dry. Stir in the cream and heat through. Remove from the heat.

Meanwhile, cook the spirals in boiling salted water until al dente, about 7 minutes. Taste test often as brands vary. Add the spirals to the sauce and toss to mix.

Divide the pasta among four heated bowls, sprinkle with the parsley, and top with the shredded cheese.

spirals with chard and garlic bread crumbs

In lieu of grated cheese, crisp, garlicky bread crumbs add flavor and texture to this rustic pasta recipe. For a vegetarian version, you can substitute chopped, oil-cured Kalamata olives for the pancetta.

SERVES 4 AS A FIRST COURSE

Warm 2 tablespoons of the olive oil in a skillet over moderate heat. Add the whole garlic clove and cook until golden, about 2 minutes.

Discard the garlic, and add the bread crumbs to the flavored oil. Using a wooden spoon, stir gently until golden brown and crisp, 1 to 2 minutes. Season with a little salt and set aside.

Warm 2 tablespoons of the remaining olive oil in a large sauté pan over moderate heat. Add the pancetta and sauté until lightly browned, 1 minute. (If using anchovies, mash them into the olive oil.)

Stir in the chopped chard stems, hot pepper flakes, and chopped garlic. Sauté for 2 minutes, reducing the heat as needed, then cover the pan and cook until the mixture is barely tender, about 7 minutes, checking and stirring often. Season with a little salt.

Meanwhile, bring a large pot of salted water to a boil, add the spirals and chard leaves, and cook until the pasta is al dente, about 7 minutes. Taste test often as brands differ.

Drain the pasta and chard, add them to the skillet and sauté for a minute or two to blend the flavors. Drizzle the remaining tablespoon of olive oil over the pasta and stir gently. Divide it among heated plates and sprinkle with the fried bread crumbs.

5 tablespoons extra-virgin olive oil

2 garlic cloves, 1 whole and 1 chopped

3/4 cup fresh white gluten-free bread crumbs (page 163)

Fine sea salt

4 tablespoons chopped pancetta (or unsmoked bacon [salt pork]) or 4 canned anchovies, chopped

Large bunch red or rainbow chard, 12 to 16 ounces, well rinsed, stems and ribs finely chopped and leaves chopped separately

Large pinch hot red pepper flakes, or more to taste

10 to 12 ounces gluten-free pasta spirals

pasta shell salad with salame, eggs, and olives

The secret to making a successful gluten-free pasta salad lies in tossing the freshly drained pasta with the dressing while still warm to better absorb the flavors and serving it within an hour or two. Refrigerating any type of cooked gluten-free pasta is not a good idea, with chilled rice flour pasta getting top place for imitating cardboard.

SERVES 4

4 large eggs

½ cup extra-virgin olive oil

2 tablespoons red wine vinegar

1 teaspoon Dijon mustard

Pinch sugar

Fine sea salt and freshly ground black pepper

6 ounces quinoa/corn pasta shells

3 ounces sliced salame, any casing removed, diced

½ cup pitted and halved lengthways Kalamata olives

½ cup halved grape tomatoes or small cherry tomatoes

2 green onions, white and pale green parts only, thinly sliced

¼ cup shredded basil leaves, or 3 tablespoons chopped flat-leaf parsley

Fine sea salt and freshly ground black pepper

Put the eggs in a saucepan and add enough cold water to cover them by ½ inch. Bring to a boil, cover, remove from the heat, and let stand for 12 minutes. They will be perfectly hard-cooked. Drain the water, crack each shell lightly on a countertop to stop the cooking, and let cool.

Whisk together the oil, vinegar, mustard, sugar, and salt and pepper to taste.

Boil the pasta shells in plenty of salted water until al dente, about 10 minutes. Brands differ, so taste test often; shells usually take longer than spaghetti or fettuccine. Drain the shells, place them in a serving bowl, toss with the dressing, and let cool.

When the pasta has reached room temperature, gently stir in the salame, olives, tomatoes, onion, and basil. Taste for seasoning, and adjust as needed. Shell the eggs and cut into wedges, season lightly with salt and pepper, and arrange on top of the salad.

penne and beans with pork ragù

Comfort food for a cold night, this combination is particularly delicious and supplies great nutrition. The ragù can be made ahead and refrigerated for up to two days, or frozen for two months.

SERVES 4

Warm the olive oil in a large, heavy pot over moderate heat. Add the pork chunks and sauté until browned, about 5 minutes. Remove with a slotted spoon and reserve.

Add the sausage to the pot and brown lightly, 1 to 2 minutes. Sprinkle with the sage and fennel seeds. Stir in the onion, celery, and garlic and cook until slightly softened, scraping up any browned bits from the bottom of the pan, about 2 minutes. Add the wine, and let bubble for 2 minutes to evaporate a little.

Return the pork to the pot and add the tomatoes. Season with salt and pepper and stir in the water. Partially cover the pan and simmer gently, stirring occasionally, until tender (add a little more water if the sauce seems dry), about 1½ hours. Stir in the beans and olives, and heat through.

Meanwhile, boil the pasta in salted water until al dente, about 7 minutes. Taste test often as brands differ. Drain the pasta.

Divide the ragù among four shallow bowls and top with the penne. Scatter the parsley and Parmesan on top.

RAGÙ

2 tablespoons extra-virgin olive oil

1 pound boneless pork shoulder, trimmed of excess fat and cut into ¾-inch chunks

1 mild Italian pork sausage (3 to 4 ounces), casing removed, chopped

1 teaspoon chopped fresh sage, or ½ teaspoon dried sage

½ teaspoon fennel seeds

1 medium yellow onion, chopped

1 rib celery, de-stringed and finely diced

2 garlic cloves, chopped

½ cup dry red wine

1 (14- to 15-ounce) can Italian plum tomatoes, quartered, juice included

Fine sea salt and freshly ground black pepper

⅓ cup water

1 (15-ounce) can white kidney beans (cannellini), rinsed and drained, or 2 cups cooked beans

⅓ cup pitted and halved lengthways Kalamata olives

8 ounces gluten-free penne, such as DeBoles multigrain penne with rice, amaranth, and quinoa

3 tablespoons chopped flat-leaf parsley

2 to 4 tablespoons grated Parmigiano-Reggiano

fresh rice flour egg pasta with butter and parmesan

This fresh egg pasta should probably come with a warning. It's addictive. It's easiest to make with a pasta machine, but rolling the dough by hand between two sheets of plastic wrap works, too. It can be cut into any width you choose: 1/4-inch wide for fettuccine, 1/2-inch to 3/4-inch wide for pappardelle, 2 inches wide for lasagne, or various shapes for ravioli. As with all fresh pasta, it cooks in 2 minutes or less. The recipe is easy to double.

MAKES APPROXIMATELY ½ POUND OF FRESH PASTA; SERVES 2

²/₃ cup (4 ounces) brown rice flour

⅓ cup (2 ounces) tapioca starch, plus extra if needed

½ teaspoon xanthan gum

½ teaspoon fine sea salt

1 large egg

1 large egg yolk

1 tablespoon extra-virgin olive oil, plus 1 teaspoon for cooking the pasta

1 tablespoon water, approximately

3 tablespoons unsalted butter, softened

2 ounces (about ½ cup) freshly grated Parmigiano-Reggiano

Combine the rice flour, tapioca starch, xanthan gum, and salt in a food processor and process to mix. Combine the egg, egg yolk, olive oil, and water in a small bowl and whisk to combine.

With the motor running, pour the egg mixture over the flour and pulse in a food processor until the dough forms into a rough ball. (If it's too wet to roll out, add about 1 tablespoon tapioca starch; if it's too dry, add a few drops of water.)

Turn out, crumbs and all, and pat together into a disk. Cut the dough in half and work with one half at a time. Enclose the other one in plastic wrap.

If using a pasta machine, see page 71. If cutting the pasta by hand, place the ball of dough between two sheets of plastic wrap and roll into a very thin, even rectangle approximately 10 x 12 inches (it should be as thin as a dime; Italian cooks say you should be able to read newspaper headlines through it), turning the sheet of dough several times. Repeat with the second ball of dough.

If using immediately, peel off the plastic, lay one sheet on a large cutting board, and cut into strips of desired width. Lay the strips on a clean kitchen towel and let them dry slightly, for about 10 minutes. If freezing the dough, leave the sheets inside the plastic wrap and cut later. (The dough may be frozen for up to 2 months.)

To cook: Bring 2 quarts of water to a rolling boil. Add 1 teaspoon of salt and the pasta. Cook, stirring occasionally, until the pasta is al dente, about 2 minutes. Drain and toss with the butter and Parmesan, or sauce of choice.

USING A PASTA MACHINE

A FIXTURE IN just about every Italian household, pasta machines can be found in most American kitchenware shops. Atlas makes a good hand-cranked model with an adjustable roller and two built-in cutters, one for linguini and the other for fettuccine. It attaches to a table or countertop with an included C-clamp.

It will take a couple of practice sessions, but once you get the hang of the procedure, you'll find that you can roll and cut fresh, tasty, gluten-free pasta very quickly, for pennies instead of dollars for the dried variety.

Organize as much counter space as possible before you start. The finished pasta has to dry flat.

Unlike pasta dough made with wheat flour, which must rest after being kneaded together to let the gluten relax (otherwise it resists being rolled out), rice flour pasta dough can be used right away.

Work with half the pasta dough at a time and rewrap the rest. Use a little cornstarch to barely coat the piece of dough, then start rolling it through the widest setting of the pasta machine. Roll it through 3 or 4 times, each time folding the length of dough in three and feeding it back through until it's smooth and even. If the sides look ragged, just tuck them in and keep folding. It helps to "catch" the emerging sheet of dough with your free hand.

Gradually reduce the width of the opening between the rollers and keep feeding the dough through until you reach the second-to-last setting. It's fine to cut the sheets in half if they become too long to manage.

Lay the sheets of pasta on a clean kitchen towel and let dry slightly, about 5 or 10 minutes. Feed the sheets through the cutter to make strips, or cut as required for fettucine, papardelle, lasagne, or ravioli. This fresh pasta is at its best if used the same day but can be frozen for up to eight weeks.

pappardelle
with smoked salmon and cream

This luxurious first course is just right for a celebration. If you're pulling out all the stops, top each serving with a dollop of red salmon caviar instead of fresh basil.

SERVES 4 AS A FIRST COURSE

1 recipe Fresh Rice Flour Egg Pasta (page 70), or 10 ounces gluten-free dried tagliatelle or fettucine

1 cup heavy cream

Pinch hot red pepper flakes

1 teaspoon finely grated lemon zest

½ cup frozen peas, thawed

Fine sea salt and freshly ground white pepper

8 ounces smoked salmon, cut in thin strips

4 tablespoons unsalted butter, cubed, softened

1 tablespoon shredded basil

Working on a large wooden cutting board or a butcher-block surface, cut the pasta into ¾-inch wide strips. Leave to dry, without overlapping, for 10 minutes or so while you prepare the sauce.

Combine the cream, hot pepper flakes, and lemon zest in a large saucepan over moderate heat. Bring to a boil, reduce the heat to medium-low, and boil gently until reduced by one-third, about 10 minutes. Add the peas, season lightly with salt and pepper, and cook for 2 minutes. Remove from the heat and stir in the smoked salmon.

Meanwhile, cook the pasta in boiling, salted water until al dente, about 2 minutes for fresh pasta or about 7 minutes for dried pasta. Drain the pasta, transfer to a heated bowl, and toss gently with the butter.

Add the sauce and mix carefully. Divide the pasta among heated plates and sprinkle with the basil.

gorgonzola ravioli with asparagus sauce

Homemade, gluten-free ravioli are wonderfully tender—far more so than the commercially available wheat flour kind, which are often too thick and doughy—and making them is definitely worth exploring. The compliments you will receive from happy gluten-challenged diners are worth the small effort!

SERVES 4 AS A FIRST COURSE

Combine the Gorgonzola, ricotta, egg yolk, and parsley in a food processor. Season lightly with salt and pepper and blend until smooth. Transfer to a small bowl. In a separate bowl, beat the egg white lightly and set out a pastry brush.

Using a ruler and a sharp knife, cut the fresh egg pasta sheets into 3½-inch squares, making 16 to 20 squares in all.

Place a rounded teaspoon of filling in the center of each square. Lightly brush around the filling with egg white. Fold the pasta over the filling to make a triangle. Expel any air bubbles (push the air toward one corner) and press the two edges together to seal.

Heat the oven to 175°F. Divide the butter among four shallow bowls and place them on a baking sheet in the oven to melt.

Bring a large pot of water to a boil and add 1 teaspoon of salt and the asparagus. Cook the asparagus until tender, about 4 minutes. Remove with tongs (reserve the pot of boiling water) and plunge into cold water to stop the cooking and preserve the color. Drain, and cut into 3-inch lengths.

Remove the baking sheet and bowls from the oven. Divide the asparagus among the bowls, turning to coat with melted butter. Sprinkle with salt and pepper and return to the oven to keep warm.

Return the pot of water to a gentle boil, adding more water if necessary to total 2 quarts. Add the ravioli a few at a time and cook until tender, about 2 minutes. They will float to the surface when done. Using a slotted spoon, transfer to the bowls containing the butter and asparagus. Top with the grated Parmesan.

2 ounces Italian Gorgonzola, diced

2 ounces whole or part-skim ricotta

1 large egg, separated

2 tablespoons chopped parsley

Fine sea salt and freshly ground black pepper

1 recipe Fresh Rice Flour Egg Pasta, page 70

4 tablespoons unsalted butter

1 teaspoon salt

½ pound pencil-thin asparagus, woody ends snapped off

4 tablespoons freshly grated Parmigiano-Reggiano

rice flour crêpes for cannelloni

Crêpes are interchangeable with homemade pasta sheets for making cannelloni. Faster to make than pasta, crêpes have the added advantage of being especially thin and tender when made with rice flour. It's best to have the milk and eggs at room temperature, as melted butter tends to solidify on contact with ingredients that are straight out of the refrigerator.

MAKES APPROXIMATELY 14 CRÊPES

2 large eggs, at room temperature

1 cup whole or part-skim milk, at room temperature

⅓ cup (2 ounces) white rice flour

⅓ cup (2 ounces) cornstarch

Pinch fine sea salt

Pinch sugar

2 tablespoons melted butter, plus extra for skillet

Combine the eggs and milk in a food processor. Add the rice flour, cornstarch, salt, and sugar and process to mix well. Transfer the batter to a bowl and stir in the butter.

Warm an 8-inch iron crêpe pan or nonstick skillet over moderate heat. Grease with a little butter. Using a small measure, pour about 3 tablespoons of the batter into the pan, swirling it by the handle to spread it over the base. When bubbles form and the edges turn golden brown, about 25 seconds, loosen the edges with a small spatula and flip.

Brown the second side lightly, about 10 seconds. The second side will remain pale. (Stir the batter often while making the crêpes.) Stack the cooked crêpes on a plate, browned side down.

Cooked crêpes keep refrigerated for two or three days or may be frozen for up to two months. (Separate them with parchment paper, then wrap airtight.)

cannelloni with spinach, ricotta, and prosciutto

This looks and tastes luxurious, but it's really simple to put together. You can make the pancake "wraps" and filling ahead of time.

SERVES 4 AS A MAIN COURSE, 8 AS A FIRST COURSE

Preheat the oven to 350°F. Grease a 9 x 13-inch shallow baking dish with butter.

Prepare or thaw the crêpes.

Combine the spinach and water in a large skillet, bring to a boil, cover, and steam until tender, about 2 minutes. Drain the spinach, squeeze it dry, and let it cool to lukewarm.

Combine the egg yolks, ricotta, prosciutto, spinach, and half the Parmesan. Season with the nutmeg, salt, and pepper, and mix well.

Lay the crêpes browned side down on a work surface. Divide the filling equally among them, spreading it evenly to within a half-inch of the borders. Roll up, cigar fashion, and lay the crêpes in the dish seam side down. Pour the cream over all. Dot the cannelloni with the butter and sprinkle with the remaining Parmesan. Bake until the crêpes are bubbling and the top starts to tinge golden, about 20 minutes. Let cool for 5 or 10 minutes before serving.

Butter for baking dish

8 Rice Flour Crêpes (page 74)

8 ounces frozen loose-pack spinach

½ cup water

2 large egg yolks

10 ounces ricotta

4 tablespoons finely chopped prosciutto

3 ounces (about ¾ cup) grated Parmigiano-Reggiano

Pinch nutmeg

Fine sea salt and freshly ground black pepper

1 cup heavy cream or half-and-half

1 tablespoon unsalted butter, cold, cut into small dice

cannelloni with tomatoes, anchovies, and cheese

Familiar pizza toppings are shown off in a different, tempting way in this Neapolitan-style recipe for rolled and filled crêpes.

SERVES 4 AS A MAIN COURSE, 8 AS A FIRST COURSE

8 Rice Flour Crêpes
(page 74)

¼ cup extra-virgin olive
oil, plus extra for
greasing dish

1 (32-ounce) can Italian
plum tomatoes,
juice included

Fine sea salt and freshly
ground black pepper

1 teaspoon sugar

1 tablespoon Pesto Sauce
(page 49), or from a jar

2 large egg yolks

12 ounces whole or
part-skim ricotta

8 canned anchovy fillets,
drained and chopped

8 oil-cured black olives,
pitted and quartered

3 ounces (about ¾ cup)
freshly grated
Parmigiano-Reggiano

Preheat the oven to 350°F. Grease a 9 x 13-inch shallow baking dish with olive oil. Prepare or thaw the crêpes.

Warm the olive oil in a heavy saucepan over moderate heat. Add the tomatoes, season lightly with salt, pepper, and the sugar. Simmer briskly, stirring occasionally, until slightly reduced and thickened, about 20 minutes. Purée half the tomato mixture with the Pesto Sauce, and reserve the remainder.

Combine the egg yolks, ricotta, anchovies, and olives and stir well to mix.

Lay the crêpes browned side down on a work surface. Spread each one with one-eighth of the plain tomato sauce. Top with the ricotta mixture, spreading it evenly to within a half-inch of the borders. Cover with about half of the Parmesan. Roll up, cigar fashion, and lay in the dish seam side down.

Pour the puréed tomato and pesto mixture over all. Top with the remaining Parmesan. Bake until bubbling and the top starts to brown, about 20 minutes. Let the crêpes cool for 5 or 10 minutes before serving.

risotto and
other grains

CONVENIENTLY FOR THE gluten-challenged, rice is not only gluten-free but forms the basis for dozens of seductive northern Italian dishes. Few can resist the allure of a creamy risotto rich with butter and Parmesan, augmented with anything from my all-time favorite, caramelized butternut squash (page 80), to unbelievably expensive fresh white Italian truffles. (Should you ever get your hands on one of these gastronomic treasures, just shave thin curls of it over a plain, creamy risotto and revel in the extravagance.)

The kind of Italian rice used for risotto—Arborio, Carnaroli, or Vialone Nano—has short, round grains that absorb flavorful broths beautifully but don't lose their shape during cooking. For a delicious whole-grain entrée that's cooked in much the same way, don't miss the brown rice and porcini mushroom combination (page 90) or the quinoa and shrimp dish (page 88) toward the end of this chapter.

artichoke-lemon risotto

True baby artichokes don't mature into large globe artichokes; they are a smaller variety that is chokeless and fully edible after trimming. Fresh ones can be hard to find, but frozen artichoke hearts work well this risotto. The broth for risotto should be kept hot, just below a simmer, so that when it's added to the rice, the mixture doesn't stop cooking.

SERVES 4 TO 6

Warm the olive oil and 2 tablespoons of the butter in a heavy saucepan over medium-low heat. Add the onion and celery and cook, stirring, until softened, about 5 minutes. Push to the edges of the pan. Increase the heat slightly and add another 2 tablespoons of butter. When it melts, add the artichoke hearts and brown them lightly, about 3 minutes.

Stir in the rice and lemon zest, stirring to coat with the oil and butter. Pour in the wine and cook briefly until almost evaporated.

Add the broth, about ½ cup at a time, stirring often and allowing the liquid to be almost absorbed before adding the next amount. Reduce the heat as needed to maintain a simmer.

Continue cooking until the rice is creamy and tender to the bite, about 25 minutes, adding a little extra hot water if needed. The rice should be creamy, not stiff or soupy. The artichokes will almost melt into the rice.

Gently stir in the remaining 4 tablespoons butter and Parmesan. Taste for seasoning, and add salt and pepper if needed. Divide the risotto among four heated shallow bowls.

1 tablespoon
extra-virgin olive oil

6 tablespoons
unsalted butter

1 small yellow onion,
finely chopped

1 celery rib, de-stringed
and finely chopped

10 ounces frozen
artichoke heart quarters,
unthawed

1½ cups Arborio rice

Zest of ½ small lemon,
cut into slivers

½ cup dry white wine,
such as Pinot Grigio

2 cups gluten-free
chicken broth or
vegetable broth mixed
with 2 cups water,
heated

1 ounce (about ¼ cup)
freshly grated
Parmigiano-Reggiano

Fine sea salt and freshly
ground black pepper

COOKING ITALIAN RISOTTO RICE

THE GENTLE ACTION of stirring a risotto releases some of the starch in round-grain Arborio, Carnaroli, and Vialone Nano rice, which is what makes a well-made risotto so creamy when cooked. (Long-grain rice turns to mush if cooked this way.) The actual cooking time varies from 20 to 30 minutes depending on the age of the rice, which gradually swells and takes on flavors but retains its shape. To test for doneness, bite into a grain; the rice is ready when it's tender but retains a slight firmness at the center.

caramelized butternut squash risotto

Butternut squash cubes become wonderfully sweet and velvety when roasted. They combine perfectly with pancetta in a creamy risotto.

SERVES 4

12-pound butternut squash, peeled, seeded, and cut into ⅓-inch dice

2 tablespoons extra-virgin olive oil

Fine sea salt and freshly ground black pepper

4 ounces pancetta or unsmoked bacon (salt pork), finely diced

1 medium yellow onion, finely chopped

1 rib celery, de-stringed and finely chopped

2 cloves garlic, chopped

1 teaspoon chopped rosemary

1 cup Arborio rice

½ cup dry white wine, such as Pinot Grigio

2 cups gluten-free chicken or vegetable broth mixed with 2 cups water, heated

2 tablespoons butter

2 ounces (about ½ cup) grated Parmigiano-Reggiano

¼ cup chopped flat-leaf parsley

Preheat the oven to 350°F. Toss the squash cubes with 1 table-spoon of the olive oil and season with salt and pepper. Roast until tender and starting to caramelize and turn golden brown, turning once, about 30 minutes.

Meanwhile, warm the remaining tablespoon of olive oil in a large sauté pan over moderate heat. Add the pancetta, onion, and celery. Cook, stirring often, until the onion softens and turns pale gold, about 7 minutes. Stir in the garlic and rosemary.

Add the rice, stirring to coat with oil. Pour in the wine and cook briefly until almost evaporated.

Add the broth, about ½ cup at a time, stirring often and allowing the liquid to be almost absorbed before adding the next amount. Continue until the rice is creamy and tender to the bite, about 25 minutes, adding a little extra hot water if needed.

Stir the butternut squash mixture into the rice. Gently stir in the butter and Parmesan. Taste for seasoning and add salt and pepper if needed. Divide the risotto among four heated shallow bowls and sprinkle with the parsley.

PREPARING A BUTTERNUT SQUASH

THIS IS A divide-and-conquer operation. Cut off the long neck that extends from the bulbous base. Using a Y-shaped vegetable peeler, peel off the skin and the pale layer immediately beneath it, down to the orange flesh. Chop into 1-inch cubes. Next, scrape the seeds out of the round end, peel, and dice.

gorgonzola risotto

As with all Italian recipes, this one depends on the quality of the ingredients, so splurge on the very best imported Gorgonzola. Lesser blue cheeses don't have its creamy, mellow richness.

SERVES 4

Warm the olive oil in a large saucepan over moderate heat. Add the onion. Cook, stirring often, until the onion softens and turns pale gold, about 7 minutes.

Add the rice, stirring to coat with oil. Add the wine and let it almost evaporate.

Stir in the chicken broth, about ½ cup at a time, stirring often and allowing the liquid to be almost absorbed before adding the next amount. Continue until the rice is creamy and tender to the bite, about 25 minutes, adding a little extra hot water if needed.

Gently stir in the Gorgonzola and Parmesan. Taste for seasoning and add salt and pepper if needed. Divide the risotto among four heated shallow bowls and sprinkle with the parsley.

2 tablespoons extra-virgin olive oil

1 medium yellow onion, finely chopped

1 cup Arborio rice

½ cup dry white wine, such as Pinot Grigio

2 cups gluten-free chicken broth mixed with 2 cups water, heated

4 ounces Gorgonzola, cut into small cubes

1 ounce (about ¼ cup) grated Parmigiano-Reggiano

Fine sea salt and freshly ground black pepper

¼ cup chopped flat-leaf parsley

spring vegetable risotto

Make this New World version of Risotto Primavera when spring vegetables finally make their appearance in the market. Cooking the baby veggies separately ensures that they don't overcook. Allow a bit of extra time for shelling the fresh fava beans and peas, which are definitely worth the trouble for their bright flavors.

SERVES 4 AS A MAIN COURSE

3 tablespoons unsalted butter

3 tablespoons extra-virgin olive oil

2 large shallots or 1 small yellow onion, finely chopped

1½ cups Arborio rice

Fine sea salt and freshly ground black pepper

½ cup dry white wine, such as Pinot Grigio

4 cups gluten-free vegetable broth, heated, plus ¼ cup broth for steaming vegetables

½ pound peas in the pod, shelled

½ pound tiny green beans, stalk ends nipped off

½ pound baby zucchini (finger size) cut in half lengthways

¼ pound miniature red, orange, and yellow bell peppers, quartered, seeds discarded

½ pound young fava beans, shelled, blanched, and skinned

Juice of 1 small lemon

4 tablespoons grated Parmigiano-Reggiano, or more to taste

Lemon wedges, for serving

Warm 1 tablespoon of the butter and 1 tablespoon of the olive oil in a heavy saucepan over moderate heat. Add the shallots and cook, stirring often, until softened but not colored, about 5 minutes.

Add the rice, stirring to coat with oil. Season with ½ teaspoon salt and a generous grinding of pepper. Pour in the wine, and cook until almost evaporated.

Add the broth, about ½ cup at a time, stirring often and allowing the liquid to be almost absorbed before adding the next amount. Reducing the heat to maintain a simmer, cook until the rice is creamy and tender to the bite, about 25 minutes, adding hot water if needed. The risotto should look very slightly soupy, not dry.

Meanwhile, heat the remaining 2 tablespoons of olive oil in a large sauté pan over moderate heat. Add the peas, green beans, zucchini, and peppers. Sauté until slightly softened, about 3 minutes. Add the remaining ¼ cup of vegetable broth, cover the pan, reduce the heat to low and cook until the vegetables are tender-crisp, about 3 minutes. Stir in the fava beans and cook for 1 minute, or until just tender.

Stir the vegetables, lemon juice, and remaining 2 tablespoons of butter gently into the rice. Taste for seasoning. Divide the risotto among four shallow bowls and top with the Parmesan. Garnish with the lemon wedges.

FAVA BEANS

ONE OF THE earliest crops to be cultivated in the Old World (and one of the easiest to grow, which might have a lot to do with it), fava beans—also known as broad beans, horse beans, and field beans—probably became part of the eastern Mediterranean diet about 6,000 years ago.

In Italy, broad beans are traditionally sown on All Souls Day, November 2. Cookies made in the shape of broad beans called *fave dei morti* or "beans of the dead" are offered on that day. As with other legumes like chickpeas and lentils, most of the crop is dried, but fresh fava beans are a beloved Italian spring food. In Rome, it's traditional to eat raw baby fava beans with Pecorino Romano cheese on May 1. They are delectable added to a salad on any spring day you choose.

Unshelled, fresh fava beans look like lumpy green beans on steroids. The pale-green pods are about 6 inches long and lined with what looks like white cotton batting, the better to shelter a row of 4 or 5 beans further encased in waxy shells. Mother nature got very protective here. Preparing them for the table takes a little time, but the results are worth it.

First string and shuck the beans. Then parboil them for 30 seconds, drain, and plunge them into cold water. Drain again, and slip off the waxy skins. You will end up with maybe 1 pound of beans for every 5 pounds of pods.

three-onion risotto

A tribute to the onion family, this fresh-tasting risotto makes an elegant main course for vegetarian guests and can double as a side dish.

SERVES 4 TO 6

1 tablespoon extra-virgin olive oil

4 tablespoons unsalted butter, divided

1 medium yellow onion, quartered and sliced

2 garlic cloves, chopped

2 medium leeks (¾ pound), white and pale-green parts only, thinly sliced, well rinsed, drained, and spun dry

1½ cups Arborio rice

Fine sea salt and freshly ground white pepper

½ cup dry white wine, such as Pinot Grigio

3 cups gluten-free vegetable broth, mixed with 1 cup water, heated

¼ cup heavy cream, at room temperature

6 green onions, white and pale-green parts only, finely chopped

2 tablespoons shredded basil or flat-leaf parsley

2 ounces (about ½ cup) grated Parmigiano-Reggiano

Warm the olive oil and half the butter in a heavy saucepan over medium-low heat. Add the onion, garlic, and leeks and cook, stirring often, until softened but not colored, about 10 minutes, reducing the heat to low if necessary.

Add the rice, stirring to coat with oil. Season with ½ teaspoon salt and a generous grinding of pepper. Pour in the wine and let it cook until almost evaporated.

Add the broth, about ½ cup at a time, stirring often and allowing the liquid to be almost absorbed before adding the next amount. Simmer gently, adjusting the heat as needed, and cook until the rice is creamy and tender to the bite, about 25 minutes, adding hot water if needed. The risotto should look very slightly soupy.

Stir in the cream, green onions, basil, remaining butter, and Parmesan. Taste and adjust seasoning as needed. Divide the risotto among four heated shallow bowls.

chicken and prosciutto risotto

A comforting, satisfying, one-dish meal for two at any time, but especially on a cold, wet night. You can substitute chicken breast meat, but if so, sauté it separately until just cooked through and stir it into the rice at the last minute. Breast meat gets dry and thready if cooked for too long.

SERVES 2

Warm the olive oil and 2 tablespoons of the butter in a heavy saucepan over moderate heat. Add the onion and garlic and cook, stirring, until softened but not colored, about 5 minutes. Add the chicken and cook, turning the pieces over often, until no longer pink, about 5 minutes. Sprinkle with the marjoram and add the prosciutto. Season with salt and pepper.

Add the rice, stirring to coat with oil. Pour in the wine and cook until almost evaporated.

Stir in 1 cup of the hot broth. Simmer gently, adjusting the heat as needed and stirring often, until the liquid is almost absorbed. Repeat with the remaining 2 cups of broth, a half cup at a time. Cook until the rice is creamy and just tender to the bite, about 25 minutes, adding extra hot water if needed. The risotto should look very slightly soupy, not dry.

Remove from the heat and stir in the parsley and remaining tablespoon of butter. Taste, and adjust seasoning as needed. Divide between two heated shallow bowls and top with the Parmesan.

1 tablespoon extra-virgin olive oil

3 tablespoons unsalted butter

1 small yellow onion, finely chopped

1 garlic clove, chopped

6 to 8 ounces skinless and boneless chicken thigh meat, cut in 1 x ½-inch chunks

½ teaspoon dried marjoram

2 tablespoons diced prosciutto or pancetta (or unsmoked bacon [salt pork])

Fine sea salt and freshly ground black pepper

1 cup Arborio rice

⅓ cup dry white wine, such as Pinot Grigio

1½ cups gluten-free chicken broth mixed with 1½ cups water, heated

3 tablespoons chopped flat-leaf parsley

2 tablespoons grated Parmigiano-Reggiano

off-the-shelf clam risotto

In Italy, rissoto alla vongole made with tiny fresh clams in the shell is a favorite coastal dish. Duplicate the briny flavors with canned American clams for a fast, savory supper.

SERVES 4

2 (6½-ounce) cans shelled Chesapeake Bay (or other) clams, juice reserved

½ cup dry white wine, such as Pinot Grigio

2 cups water, approximately

2 tablespoons extra-virgin olive oil

6 tablespoons diced pancetta or unsmoked bacon (salt pork)

1 small yellow onion, finely chopped

¼ teaspoon saffron threads

1½ cups Arborio rice

Juice of 1 small lemon

½ cup chopped flat-leaf parsley

Fine sea salt and freshly ground black pepper

Combine the clam juice from the cans with ¼ cup of the wine and enough water to make 4 cups and bring to a very gentle simmer. Keep warm.

Warm the olive oil in a large sauté pan over medium-low heat. Add the pancetta and onion. Cook, stirring often, until the onion softens and turns pale gold, about 5 minutes. Crumble the saffron into the pan between your fingers.

Add the rice, stirring to coat with oil. Add the remaining ¼ cup wine and let it almost evaporate.

Add the hot clam broth, about ½ cup at a time, stirring often and allowing the liquid to be almost absorbed before adding the next amount. Continue until the rice is creamy and tender to the bite, about 25 minutes, adding a little extra hot water if needed. The finished rice should look a little soupy, not dry.

Shortly before the rice is ready, stir the clam meat into the rice so it can heat through. Be careful not to overheat or the clams will toughen. Stir in the lemon juice and parsley. Taste for seasoning, and add salt and pepper if needed. Divide the risotto among four heated shallow bowls.

upside-down risotto

Some cooks aver that you can't reheat risotto, but that's not so. Venetian cooks long ago invented risotto al salto ("somersault"), a kind of buttery, golden, rice fritatta that's wonderful served for a light meal with salad. Leftover risotto from any of those given in this chapter will do nicely, except the two cheese-free seafood ones (Off-the-Shelf Clam Risotto and Quinoa Risotto with Shrimp).

SERVES 2

Using a fork, beat the egg in a mixing bowl. Blend in the risotto and Parmesan. Season lightly with salt and pepper.

Warm the butter in an 8-inch nonstick skillet over medium-low heat. Add the rice mixture and spread it out to cover the pan base. Reduce the heat slightly, and cook until bubbles appear around the edges and the underside is firm and golden brown, about 3 minutes.

Loosen the edges with a spatula, and shake the pan gently to make sure the rice cake will come loose. Protecting your hands with oven mitts, place a flat plate over the surface and reverse both pan and plate, so the rice cake can drop out browned side up. Slide back into the pan and continue cooking until the second side is golden brown, about 2 minutes.

Slide out onto a warmed platter. Cut in wedges to serve.

TIP: You can also divide this mixture into patties and cook them in a large skillet, turning them over with a spatula.

1 large egg

1 cup leftover risotto, cold

1 ounce (about ¼ cup) grated Parmigiano-Reggiano

Fine sea salt and freshly ground black pepper

1 tablespoon unsalted butter

quinoa risotto with shrimp

Strictly speaking, a risotto must by definition be made with round-grain Italian rice, but quinoa makes a delicious whole-grain alternative that can be cooked in just the same way. The seafood and mushrooms are augmented with cream to give a voluptuous texture.

SERVES 4

1½ cups quinoa, rinsed and drained

1 tablespoon grape seed oil or canola oil

4 tablespoons unsalted butter

1 large shallot (about 2 ounces), finely sliced

2 tablespoons diced pancetta or unsmoked bacon (salt pork)

¼ pound white button mushrooms, sliced

½ cup dry white wine, such as Pinot Grigio

1 (8-ounce) bottle clam juice

½ cup heavy cream

Fine sea salt and freshly ground black pepper

¾ pound medium raw shrimp, shelled and deveined

¼ teaspoon hot red pepper flakes, or more to taste

2 tablespoons chopped flat-leaf parsley

Lemon wedges

Bring a large pot of salted water to a boil. Rinse the quinoa, drain it, and boil it, uncovered, until the white germ rings show, 8 to 10 minutes. Taste test to make sure it's tender. Drain well, spread on a rimmed baking sheet, and let dry for 30 minutes.

Warm the grape seed oil and 2 tablespoons of the butter in a sauté pan over moderate heat. When it foams, add the shallot and sauté until translucent, about 2 minutes. Add the pancetta and mushrooms and sauté until the mushrooms are glassy-looking, about 5 minutes.

Add the wine, increase the heat slightly, and let the liquid reduce by half. Stir in half (4 fluid ounces) of the clam juice and simmer the mixture for 5 minutes. Stir in the cream. When it reaches a brisk simmer, stir in the quinoa. Heat through, adding a little more clam juice if needed to keep the mixture from becoming dry. Remove from the heat. Taste, and add salt and pepper as needed.

Warm the remaining 2 tablespoons of butter in a large skillet over moderate heat. When it foams, add the shrimps and hot pepper flakes. Sauté until opaque and cooked through, about 2 minutes. Season lightly with salt and pepper, and stir into the quinoa. Add the parsley and divide the risotto among four heated plates. Garnish with the lemon wedges.

TIP: You will have about half a bottle of clam juice left over. Freeze it in a small, screw-topped glass jar for another day, leaving enough headroom for expansion.

COOKING QUINOA

THE INSTRUCTIONS ON boxes of quinoa tell you to cook the grains covered with 2 parts water to 1 part quinoa, but this tends to make the grains too soft, especially if you plan to dry the quinoa before incorporating it into a risotto or pilaf-style dish.

In Peru, the chefs at Lima's top restaurants—which are extremely elegant and sophisticated—are more likely to cook quinoa uncovered in lots of boiling water for 8 to 10 minutes, drain it as soon as the white germ ring shows, and let it dry before incorporating it into a risotto-like dish. As they know what they're doing with their native grain, I use the same procedure.

If you want to cook quinoa for a quick side dish, use a ratio of 1 cup quinoa to a scant 1¾ cups water or gluten-free broth. Bring the liquid to a boil and add the rinsed and drained quinoa, an optional pat of butter, and a large pinch of salt if needed. (Broths are usually presalted.) When it returns to the boil, cover the pot, reduce the heat to low, and simmer until the liquid has been absorbed and the grains are tender, about 12 minutes. Stir and let stand, covered, for 5 minutes. The cooked quinoa will swell to about 3 cups worth.

baked brown rice risotto with mushrooms

An exceptional grain dish, this one stars nutritious round-grain brown rice instead of Italian rice. (Be sure to get stubby brown rice; long-grain rice turns mushy if cooked this way.) A great dish for casual entertaining, it's easy to multiply.

SERVES 4 TO 6

Preheat the oven to 350°F.

½ ounce dried porcini mushrooms

1 cup hot water

2 tablespoons extra-virgin olive oil

5 tablespoons unsalted butter

1 medium yellow onion, finely chopped

1½ cups short- or medium-grain brown rice

½ cup dry white wine, such as Pinot Grigio

Fine sea salt and freshly ground black pepper

2 cups gluten-free chicken or vegetable broth, mixed with 1 cup water, boiling

¾ pound white and/or brown mushrooms, sliced

⅓ cup heavy cream

4 tablespoons chopped parsley

2 ounces (about ½ cup) grated Parmigiano-Reggiano

Soak the dried porcini in the hot water for 15 minutes. Lift out with a slotted spoon, reserving the liquid. Rinse in cold water to dislodge any remaining sand, chop finely, and set aside. Strain the liquid through a paper towel and add it to the hot broth.

Warm 1 tablespoon of the olive oil and 1 tablespoon of the butter in a heavy ovenproof casserole over medium-low heat. Add the onion and cook, stirring, until softened, about 5 minutes. Add the rice, stirring to coat with oil. Pour in the wine and cook until evaporated. Season with salt and pepper. Stir in the broth, increase the heat to high, and bring to a boil. Cover the casserole, transfer to the oven, and bake until the rice is tender, about 45 minutes.

About 15 minutes before the rice is done, warm the remaining tablespoon of olive oil and butter in a large skillet over moderate heat. Add the chopped porcini and sliced mushrooms and sauté until the mushrooms turn glassy-looking, about 5 minutes. Add the cream and parsley, heat gently, and season with salt and pepper.

Remove from the heat. Stir the mushroom mixture into the rice. Stir in the Parmesan. Taste, and adjust seasoning if needed. Divide the risotto among shallow bowls.

faux farro

Farro, a primitive form of wheat, was introduced into Italy after Julius Caesar's conquest of grain-rich Egypt in 30 B.C. The new and desirable "Pharaoh's grain" became known as farro and gave rise to the Italian word for flour, farina. Farro contains gluten, so it's off-limits for the gluten-intolerant. However, a combination of brown rice and quinoa provides a similar rustic, chewy texture, great taste, and lots of good nutrition. It makes a mellow side dish for meat or chicken.

MAKES 3 CUPS; SERVES 4 TO 6

Combine the chicken broth and water in a saucepan and bring to a boil over high heat. Stir in the brown rice, cover the pan, and reduce the heat to low. Let simmer for 25 minutes then stir in the rinsed and drained quinoa and a pinch of salt. (Use more if the broth is unsalted.)

Cover and simmer for a further 12 to 15 minutes, until the rice and quinoa are tender. If any liquid remains, boil hard to evaporate, stirring constantly. Taste, and add black pepper and more salt if needed.

2 cups gluten-free chicken broth or vegetable broth

1 cup water

$3/4$ cup brown rice

$3/4$ cup quinoa, well rinsed

Fine sea salt and freshly ground black pepper

tortino with eggs and cheese

Somewhat like a fritatta, this savory appetizer was originally made with farro, an ancient form of wheat that's been cultivated in Italy for 2,000 years. A brown rice–quinoa blend (Faux Farro, previous page 91) makes a very satisfactory gluten-free alternative. Serve in wedges with a handful of arugula or mixed baby greens.

SERVES 6 AS AN APPETIZER; 2 AS A MAIN COURSE

2 large eggs

2 ounces fresh white goat cheese, crumbled

2 ounces (about ½ cup) freshly grated Parmigiano-Reggiano

2 cups cooked Faux Farro, cold (page 91)

2 tablespoons finely chopped green onion, white and pale-green parts only

Fine sea salt and freshly ground black pepper

1 tablespoon unsalted butter

Using a fork, beat the eggs lightly in a large bowl. Blend in the goat cheese and Parmesan. Add the Faux Farro and green onion and season with the salt and pepper, remembering that some of the other ingredients are salty.

Warm the butter in an 8-inch nonstick or well-seasoned iron skillet over medium-low heat. Add the grain mixture and flatten slightly to cover the pan base. Reduce the heat a little and cook until the under surface is firm and golden brown, about 6 minutes.

Loosen the edges with a spatula and shake the pan gently to make sure the tortino will come loose. Protecting your hands with oven mitts, place a flat plate over the surface and reverse both pan and plate, so it can plop out browned side up. Slide back into the pan, and continue cooking until the second side is golden brown, about 3 minutes.

Reverse onto a plate, as before. Cut in wedges to serve.

WHAT'S A TORTINO?

ITALIAN CULINARY TERMS can be confusing. Just for the record:

a *torta* can be a pie, a cake, or a tart

a *tòrtano* is a ring-shaped Easter bread from Naples

a *tortina* is a small tart

a *tortino* is a savory grain "pie," usually cooked in a skillet

a *tortoni* is an ice cream cake coated with amaretti (almond cookie) crumbs, first created by an Italian chef named Tortoni who presided over a popular restaurant in nineteenth-century Paris. (See recipe on page 191.)

polenta and gnocchi

W E THINK OF polenta as being made exclusively from corn and therefore being naturally gluten-free. In fact, even though polenta has been a basic foodstuff in Italy for well over 2,000 years, it wasn't made from corn until about 400 years ago, following Columbus's discovery of the New World—and unfamiliar foods such as corn, tomatoes, and chocolate. Before then, the Italian population utilized ground millet, spelt, farro, buckwheat, chickpeas, or fava beans to make their life-sustaining porridge, which the ancient Romans called *pulmentum*.

Wonderfully versatile, polenta is to Northern Italy what pasta is to the South. It can be soft or firm and takes the place of everything from our mashed potatoes to crispy oven fries (see the recipe on page 104). It tastes delicious simply topped with melted butter and freshly grated Parmesan or with any of the pasta sauces in Chapter 3. In addition, when cooked, cooled, and sliced, polenta can substitute for toasted bread crostini or cut into shapes and baked to make Roman-style gnocchi (page 102).

basic polenta

Traditionally, coarse-ground corn for polenta was cooked in a big cast-iron pot suspended over an open fire and took about an hour of patient stirring. Fortunately for us, there are now quicker ways to make what might be called the popular Italian equivalent of mashed potatoes.

This recipe calls for express polenta as it's the most convenient and has good flavor and texture, but if you prefer to use regular polenta, just cook it for longer—about 30 minutes. (See the recipe for Polenta with Rich Tomato Sauce on page 97.)

SERVES 4

Pour the water into a 2-quart saucepan and bring to a boil. Add the salt.

Pour the polenta slowly into the boiling water and stir briskly with a whisk until the mixture returns to a boil. Reduce the heat to low, switch to a wooden spoon, and cook, stirring often, until the mixture is creamy and thick and starts to pull away from the sides of the pan, about 7 minutes.

Stir in the butter, and serve at once. Alternatively, spread out ½ inch thick on an ungreased baking sheet and let cool for later grilling or frying.

VARIATION: Use gluten-free chicken broth instead of water, or half of each, and cut back on added salt if the broth is already seasoned.

TIP: Cooked polenta tends to leave a stuck-on film in the pan, but it soaks off easily with plain water.

4 cups water

2 teaspoons fine sea salt

1 cup quick-cooking polenta, such as Beretta Express

2 tablespoons unsalted butter

quick polenta
with goat cheese and prosciutto

Fast and flavorful, all this dish needs is a green salad and a glass of wine to make a satisfying supper.

SERVES 2 AS A MAIN COURSE

3 ounces fresh white goat cheese, crumbled

1 roasted red bell pepper, from a jar is fine, drained and chopped

4 cups gluten-free chicken broth, or 2 cups broth and 2 cups water

Fine sea salt, optional

1 cup quick-cooking polenta, such as Beretta Express

Pinch fine sea salt

1 tablespoon unsalted butter, softened

2 to 3 tablespoons milk or heavy cream

2 large slices prosciutto, chopped

2 tablespoons freshly grated Parmigiano-Reggiano, or to taste

Preheat the oven to very low, about 170°F.

Mix and divide the goat cheese and bell pepper between 2 shallow bowls and put them in the oven to warm.

In a heavy saucepan, bring the chicken broth to a boil. (Add salt if using water.)

Slowly pour in the polenta and stir briskly with a whisk until the mixture returns to a boil. Reduce the heat to low, switch to a wooden spoon, and cook, stirring often, until the mixture is creamy and thick and starts to pull away from the sides of the pan, about 7 minutes. Stir in the butter and milk.

Pour the polenta over the goat cheese and pepper, and sprinkle with the prosciutto. Top with the Parmesan.

polenta with rich tomato sauce

There's more than one way to cook polenta! Most Italian cooks sprinkle cornmeal slowly into boiling water to avoid creating lumps, and then stir until it's ready, but as outlined below, you can also mix cornmeal with cold water to make a slurry, incorporate this into the boiling water, cover the pan, and let the polenta cook itself. This method gives you time to focus on making the quick but memorable sauce.

SERVES 4

Measure the polenta and salt into a small bowl. Bring the chicken broth and 1 cup of the water to a boil in a heavy saucepan.

Add the remaining cup of water to the polenta and mix well. Pour this mixture into the boiling liquid and bring to a boil, stirring constantly with a whisk. Reduce the heat to very low, cover the pan, and simmer, stirring occasionally with a wooden spoon, until the polenta is creamy and thick, about 30 minutes. If it gets too stiff, stir in a little more water.

Meanwhile, warm the olive oil in a large skillet over moderate heat. Add the onion and sauté until softened, about 3 minutes. Add the pancetta and cook until lightly browned, stirring often, about 3 minutes more. Stir in the tomatoes and fennel seeds, add a little salt and a generous grinding of pepper, and simmer over low heat until slightly thickened, about 15 minutes. Taste, and add salt and pepper as needed.

Spoon the polenta onto plates, top with the sauce, and sprinkle with the Parmesan.

TIP: This sauce is equally good tossed with gluten-free pasta.

1 cup medium-grind polenta, preferably stone-ground

1 teaspoon fine sea salt

2 cups gluten-free chicken broth

2 cups water

RICH TOMATO SAUCE

2 tablespoons extra-virgin olive oil

1 medium yellow onion, chopped

2 ounces chopped pancetta or unsmoked bacon (salt pork)

1 (14- to 15-ounce) can chopped Italian plum tomatoes, juice included

$1/4$ teaspoon fennel seeds

Fine sea salt and freshly ground black pepper

4 tablespoons grated Parmigiano-Reggiano, or more to taste

no-stir baked polenta

Baking polenta is a wonderfully easy way to cook it that gives consistent results. If you're multiplying the recipe for a hungry horde, you can bake it in a roasting pan instead of a baking dish.

SERVES 4

1 cup medium-grind polenta

Fine sea salt and freshly ground black pepper

2 tablespoons butter, cut up

2 cups gluten-free chicken or vegetable broth mixed with 2 cups water, heated

2 ounces (about ½ cup) freshly grated Parmigiano-Reggiano

Preheat the oven to 350°F.

Pour the polenta into an 8-cup baking dish or ovenproof skillet. Add about 1 teaspoon salt, a generous grinding of black pepper, and the butter. Stir in the hot broth, and transfer to the oven. Bake for 35 minutes, uncovered.

Stir well, add the Parmesan, and bake for a further 10 minutes. Let rest for 5 minutes before serving with whatever topping you choose.

Alternatively, if you plan to slice and fry the polenta later, grease an 8 x 4-inch loaf pan with olive oil. Pour in the hot polenta and smooth the top. Let cool, cover, and refrigerate for at least 3 hours. Slice ½ inch thick.

TIP: Leftover cooked and cooled polenta can be finely diced and added to minestrone or other hearty soups instead of pasta.

off-the-shelf polenta crostini with caramelized red onion

Precooked rolls of polenta have a rather bland flavor and texture, but they're unde-niably useful. Of course, if you happen to have chilled home-cooked polenta waiting in your refrigerator, so much the better. These polenta crostini can serve as an appe-tizer or first course, and the recipe is easy to double.

SERVES 6 AS AN APPETIZER

Cut twelve ½-inch thick slices off the polenta roll. (Refrigerate the remainder for another use.)

Heat the olive oil in a heavy saucepan over moderate heat. Add the onions and sprinkle with the sugar. Reduce the heat to low and cook, stirring often, until soft and golden, about 20 minutes. Increase the heat slightly, add the red wine vinegar, and stir until it evaporates, about 30 seconds. Repeat with the balsamic vinegar. Season to taste with salt and pepper.

Heat a nonstick skillet over moderate heat. Spray or brush one side of the polenta slices with olive oil and fry until crisp and starting to brown, about 4 minutes. Spray again with oil, turn, and brown the second side, about 3 minutes.

Spoon about 1 teaspoon of the onion mixture on each round of polenta, spreading it out slightly. Top with the Parmesan. Serve warm.

TIP: Find more crostini toppings in Chapter 9.

1 (18-ounce) roll precooked polenta, or 12 ½-inch thick, 2½-inch diameter rounds of precooked and chilled polenta

2 tablespoons extra-virgin olive oil

2 red onions (about 1 pound), quartered and thinly sliced

1 tablespoon sugar

2 tablespoons red wine vinegar

1 tablespoon balsamic vinegar

Fine sea salt and freshly ground black pepper

Olive oil spray

3 tablespoons grated Parmigiano-Reggiano or Pecorino Romano

spinach and ricotta gnocchi with sage butter

Italian potato gnocchi (nyo-kee) are small poached dumplings served as a first course. The amount of potato they contain varies according to region; at the lower end of the scale, they can be little sinkers! These gnocchi are of the elegant variety—see opposite page for cooking tips. This recipe makes about thirty oval dumplings.

SERVES 4

2 medium (1-pound) baking potatoes, such as Russets or Idaho, unpeeled

1 bunch spinach, preferably organic (about 12 ounces), de-stemmed, well rinsed, and drained or enough cooked, drained, and squeezed frozen spinach to make ½ cup

4 ounces ricotta

4 ounces (about 1 cup) grated Parmigiano-Reggiano, plus extra at the table

1 large egg

1 large egg yolk

Pinch freshly grated nutmeg

¼ teaspoon xanthan gum

2 tablespoons white rice flour, plus more for dusting

Fine sea salt and freshly grated black pepper

4 tablespoons butter, plus more for greasing dish

10 sage leaves, chopped

Preheat the oven to 375°F. Prick the potatoes and bake until soft, about 50 minutes. When cool enough to handle, cut in half and scoop out the insides, discarding the "shells." Push through a potato ricer or coarse sieve into a mixing bowl.

Pile the spinach into a large pot with just the water that clings to the leaves, cover, and cook over moderate heat until thoroughly wilted, about 5 minutes. Drain well, and when cool enough to handle, squeeze dry and chop finely. You should have about ½ cup.

Add the spinach to the riced potatoes. Using a wooden spoon, beat in the ricotta, ¾ cup of the Parmesan, the egg, egg yolk, nutmeg, xanthan gum, rice flour, and salt and pepper to taste.

Grease an 8 x 12-inch shallow baking dish with butter, heat it briefly, and set by the stove. Bring a large pot of water to a brisk simmer (not a rolling boil).

Sprinkle about ¼ cup white rice flour onto a plate. Using your fingers or a tablespoon, and working with five or six at a time, detach walnut-size bits of the gnocchi mixture and gently form them into 2-inch-long ovals. Place on the rice flour.

Roll the gnocchi lightly in the flour and drop in the simmering water. Cook until they float to the surface and become barely firm, about 4 minutes. Remove them with a slotted spoon and return them to the baking dish.

Repeat with the remaining gnocchi. The gnocchi can be prepared ahead to this point and kept at room temperature, covered, for an hour or two.

Preheat the oven to 375°F.

Melt the butter with the sage in a small saucepan over low heat. Pour over the gnocchi and top with the remaining ¼ cup of Parmesan. Bake until the cheese melts and browns lightly, about 5 minutes. Serve at once, passing additional Parmesan at the table.

PRODUCING LIGHT GNOCCHI

WHEN MAKING POTATO-BASED gnocchi, there are secrets to making them light and delicate. It's vital that the potatoes be floury bakers, not waxy ones like Yukon Gold, which would make the gnocchi gummy. Be sure to have the potato and spinach slightly warm when you assemble the gnocchi; the other ingredients should be at room temperature, not cold. Bake the potatoes rather than boiling them, and do not wrap them in foil, which creates steam. The potatoes must be nice and dry. Finally, using a little xanthan gum instead of a lot of flour to hold them together is key, and they must be poached gently.

baked teff gnocchi

Teff flour mixed with instant cornmeal makes a highly successful gluten-free alternative to the semolina (durum wheat granules) used in traditional baked Roman-style gnocchi. It is easy to work with as it sets up firmly, and it has a rich flavor.

SERVES 4 AS A FIRST COURSE

½ cup teff flour, such as Bob's Red Mill

½ cup instant polenta, such as Beretta

6 tablespoons unsalted butter, plus extra for baking dish

2 cups milk mixed with 2 cups water

2 teaspoons fine sea salt

3 ounces (about ¾ cup) grated Parmigiano-Reggiano

1 large egg yolk

Combine the teff flour and polenta and set aside. Melt 4 tablespoons of the butter in a heavy saucepan over medium-low heat. Using a wooden spoon, stir in the teff flour mixture and keep stirring for a few seconds until it resembles damp sand.

Add the milk little by little, stirring briskly to keep the mixture smooth. Add the salt and continue stirring until the mixture becomes very thick, leaves the sides of the pan, and forms a shiny-looking ball, about 5 minutes.

Remove the pan from the heat. Stir in ½ cup of the Parmesan and the egg yolk. Spoon the dough onto a baking sheet and spread it into a ½-inch thickness with a metal spatula. When it cools down a little, which is almost immediately, you can finish patting the dough smooth and flat with your palm. As the dough sets up so well, you can cut out the gnocchi immediately or let the dough cool and refrigerate it, covered, for up to 24 hours.

Preheat the oven to 400°F. Grease a 13 x 9-inch shallow baking dish with butter.

Using a 1½-inch cookie cutter, cut out rounds of the dough (or simply cut into 1½-inch squares) and arrange them in the baking dish. Slightly overlapping the gnocchi is fine.

Melt the remaining 2 tablespoons of butter and drizzle over the gnocchi. Sprinkle with the remaining ¼ cup of Parmesan. Bake until golden and bubbling, 15 to 20 minutes. Let cool for a few minutes before serving.

TIP: These savory little Parmesan-topped rounds can double as warm appetizers. Bake without overlapping, and place 3 or 4 per serving on small plates. (The recipe makes about 40).

fried polenta sandwiches

An Italian-style variation on the classic toasted cheese sandwich, these quick and easy snacks are always popular for lunch. Serve with a green salad.

SERVES 4

Cut the polenta roll into sixteen slices, about ⅓-inch thick, discarding the rounded ends.

Tuck slices of cheese and two or three pieces of prosciutto between two rounds of polenta, making eight small sandwiches. Press each one lightly together. Dip the sandwiches in the flour, then in the beaten egg, and finally in the breadcrumbs.

Warm the olive oil in a large, heavy skillet over moderate heat and fry the polenta sandwiches on both sides until golden brown, about 5 minutes total. Drain on paper towels, and serve hot. (The sandwiches may be kept warm in a low oven for 10 minutes.)

VARIATION: Substitute thinly sliced ham, trimmed into 2½-inch diameter rounds, for the prosciutto.

1 roll (16 ounces) precooked polenta

3 ounces Fontina or Gruyère, thinly sliced with a cheese slicer or vegetable peeler

2 ounces prosciutto, thinly sliced and cut in thirds or quarters

¼ cup white rice flour, for dusting

1 large egg, lightly beaten

1 cup Homemade Bread Crumbs (page 163)

¼ cup extra-virgin olive oil

polenta oven fries

Golden-brown and crispy on the outside and soft within, polenta "French fries" make a popular snack with a glass of wine, or a side dish with just about anything.

SERVES 4 TO 6

6 cups water

1 teaspoon fine sea salt

1½ cups quick-cooking polenta, such as Beretta Express

3 ounces (about ¾ cup) grated Pecorino Romano

4 tablespoons unsalted butter, softened

Fine sea salt and freshly ground black pepper

Olive oil spray

Bring the water to a boil and add the salt.

Add the polenta in a steady stream, stirring all the while with a wire whisk to prevent lumps. Switch to a wooden spoon, reduce the heat to low, and continue stirring until the polenta thickens and pulls away from the side of the pan, about 7 minutes.

Remove the pan from the heat and stir in the pecorino and butter. Season with salt and pepper to taste and stir until smooth. Pour onto an ungreased baking sheet and spread to a thickness of about ¾ inch. Let the polenta cool and refrigerate it for at least 2 hours.

Preheat the oven to 400°F. Cut the polenta into 3 ½-inch long batons. Line a large baking sheet with aluminum foil and arrange the "fries" on it, ½ inch apart. Spray them with olive oil, turn over, and spray again. Bake the fries until golden-brown and crispy, turning once, about 30 minutes total.

birds

G REAT ITALIAN POULTRY recipes go back a long way. According to ancient texts, wealthy Romans were fattening chickens for the table on wine-soaked raisins 2,000 years ago. It's still a great flavor combination—see the recipe for Winemaker's Chicken with Raisins on page 111.

We're fortunate to have plump chickens and turkeys so readily available in the United States, but if possible, do buy humanely raised organic or free-range birds. They not only have far nicer lives—and taste superior—but it's better for your long-term health as they don't consume suspect additives with their feed.

Chicken provides a great canvas for gluten-free artistry. Depending on the other ingredients you have on hand, from almond meal and an egg for coating breast meat scaloppine (page 108) to a handful of olives for stuffing roast chicken legs (page 110), chicken can be transformed into a totally different meal.

chicken breast skewers
with quinoa risotto

Ideal for casual summer entertaining, spiedini (kebabs) cook fast, look appetizing, and taste wonderful. Start with the quinoa as it has to dry before cooking. (For different ways to cook quinoa, see page 89.)

SERVES 4

Bring a large pot of salted water to a boil, add the quinoa, and cook uncovered until just tender and the white germ rings show, 8 to 10 minutes. Drain well, spread out on a baking sheet, and let dry for at least 30 minutes.

Meanwhile, place the chicken chunks and chopped marjoram in a bowl, add the olive oil, and season lightly with salt and pepper. Turn the chunks to coat them with the oil and let them stand for 20 minutes. Wrap the chicken chunks in strips of coppa and thread onto 8 skewers alternately with the tomatoes.

Warm the butter in a large skillet over moderate heat. When it foams, add the onion and garlic and cook, stirring often, until softened but not colored, about 5 minutes. Add the quinoa and stir well to coat. Add the wine and let it evaporate. Stir in the broth and simmer for a further 5 minutes. Add the cream and parsley and heat through. Add the Parmesan. Taste for seasoning and add salt and/or pepper if needed.

In the meantime, heat the broiler. Place the chicken skewers about 3 inches from the heat and broil until just cooked through, about 3 minutes per side. Spoon the quinoa risotto onto a heated platter and top with the chicken skewers. Serve warm, not blazing hot.

QUINOA RISOTTO

Fine sea salt

1 cup quinoa, rinsed and drained

2 tablespoons unsalted butter

1 small onion, finely chopped

1 garlic clove, finely chopped

1/4 cup dry white wine, such as Pinot Grigio

1/2 cup gluten-free chicken broth

4 to 6 tablespoons heavy cream

2 tablespoons chopped flat-leaf parsley

2 ounces (about 1/2 cup) grated Parmigiano-Reggiano

CHICKEN SKEWERS

1 pound chicken breast meat, boneless and skinless, cut into 1-inch chunks

1 tablespoon chopped fresh marjoram or oregano

1 tablespoon extra-virgin olive oil

Fine sea salt and freshly ground black pepper

12 thin slices coppa (available vacuum-packed in many supermarkets and sliced to order in Italian delis) or pancetta (or unsmoked bacon [salt pork]), each cut into 3 strips

3/4 pound small red grape tomatoes

chicken scaloppine with almond crust and lemon

Milanese cooks prepare veal scaloppine (cutlets) this way; the recipe also works with chicken breast. A side dish of green beans or asparagus goes well here.

SERVES 4

1 pound chicken breast meat, sliced ⅓-inch thick (see below)

Fine sea salt and freshly ground black pepper

¼ cup white rice flour

1 large egg, beaten

½ cup almond meal

6 tablespoons unsalted butter

2 tablespoons chopped flat-leaf parsley

Lemon wedges to garnish

Season the chicken cutlets with a little salt and pepper. Dip them first in flour, then in beaten egg, and finally in the almond meal.

Melt the butter in a large skillet over moderate heat. When it sizzles, add the cutlets in one layer, without crowding. (Do this in batches or divide the cutlets between two pans.) Cook the cutlets on both sides until golden, reducing the heat a little as needed, about 4 minutes in all. Turn the cutlets once more before serving, and transfer them to four warmed plates. Garnish with the parsley and lemon wedges.

SLICING RAW CHICKEN BREAST

MAKING SCALOPPINE FROM a large boned and skinned half-breast of chicken is easy when you know how. Set it skin (curved) side up on a cutting board. Rest one hand on top, fingers stretched out flat and slightly upwards. Using a sharp paring knife, carefully cut the meat horizontally, steadying it under your palm, making 2 or 3 thin slices (cutlets) depending on the size of the chicken breast.

chicken scaloppine with summer tomato sauce

When made at the height of summer with flagrantly ripe and flavorful fresh tomatoes and fresh oregano, this familiar combination turns into a new dish altogether. A side dish of long-grain white rice cooked in chicken broth makes a perfect accompaniment.

SERVES 4

Prepare the chicken breasts. Just before cooking, dredge the cutlets lightly in the rice flour.

Warm the olive oil in a large skillet over medium-low heat. Brown the cutlets on both sides until just cooked through, about 2 minutes total. Season lightly with salt and pepper and transfer to a plate. Don't worry if the meat looks rather pale.

Add the wine to the pan, scraping up any residue on the bottom with a wooden spoon, and let it almost evaporate. Add the tomatoes, sugar, and oregano. Cook until softened but not mushy, about 5 minutes. Return the cutlets to the pan and add the capers. Turn the cutlets over once or twice to coat with the sauce, and heat through, about 1 minute. Divide the chicken among four heated dinner plates and garnish with oregano sprigs if using.

1 pound skinless chicken breast meat, sliced horizontally into ⅓-inch thick cutlets (see page 108)

¼ cup white rice flour

2 tablespoons extra-virgin olive oil

Fine sea salt and freshly ground black pepper

½ cup dry white wine

2 cups diced, vine-ripened tomatoes, juice included

1 teaspoon sugar

1 teaspoon chopped fresh oregano, or ½ teaspoon dried

1 tablespoon capers, rinsed and drained

Oregano sprigs, optional

roast chicken legs
with olive stuffing

Chopped olive spread, generally marketed as tapenade, lends lively flavor to chicken legs when combined with gluten-free bread crumbs and parsley and stuffed under the skin. The skin turns brown and crisp, but the meat stays moist and juicy. For an easy side dish, serve caramelized grape tomatoes (see Caramelized Grape Tomato Crostini, page 171) with a handful of arugula or baby spinach leaves.

SERVES 4

4 whole chicken legs, 6 to 8 ounces each

4 tablespoons black olive paste (see Olive Paste Bruschetta, page 170), or purchased tapenade

1 cup Homemade Bread Crumbs (page 163)

4 tablespoons chopped parsley

1 tablespoon butter, softened

Freshly ground black pepper

Preheat the oven to 375°F. Line a rimmed baking sheet with aluminum foil to save clean-up time.

Using a heavy knife, chop off the knobby end of each drumstick and pull out and cut off as much of the tough white tendons as possible. (This step makes the drumstick meat much nicer to eat: no chewy bits.) Using your fingers, gently separate the skin from the flesh of each chicken leg, reaching in as far as possible but leaving it attached at the sides. If the skin comes loose, secure with a poultry pin or toothpick after stuffing.

Combine the olive paste, bread crumbs, and the parsley. Insert this mixture under the skin of each chicken leg, pushing it as far as possible down the drumstick. Spread the stuffing out by "massaging" the skin. (Don't stuff the under surface; just the top.) Arrange the chicken legs on the baking sheet, spaced well apart. Spread each one with ¼ of the butter and sprinkle with black pepper. Roast the chicken legs until golden-brown and cooked through, about 40 minutes. Let cool for a few minutes before serving.

winemaker's chicken with raisins

Red wine and dried grapes lend a bit of Tuscan magic to chicken thigh meat, which stays juicy and succulent when simmered gently.

SERVES 6

Pull the skin off the chicken thighs and discard. Trim off any excess fat. Roll each thigh in the rice flour to coat evenly, shaking off any excess.

Warm the olive oil in a large sauté pan over moderate heat. Add the chicken and brown on both sides, in two batches if necessary, about 7 minutes. Transfer to a plate, and season with salt and pepper.

Add the wine to the pan and stir with a wooden spoon to loosen any stuck browned bits. Add the broth, the hot pepper flakes, shallots, raisins, garlic, tomato paste, pancetta, and brandy.

Return the chicken to the pan, turning the pieces to coat well. Cover, reduce the heat to low, and simmer for 20 minutes. Turn the chicken thighs over. If the sauce seems to be evaporating too fast, add a little more chicken broth. Cover the pan and continue cooking until the chicken is fork tender and the sauce is reduced to about 1½ cups. Conversely, if there's too much sauce, remove the chicken and boil hard to reduce.

6 large chicken thighs, with bone, about 3 pounds

¼ cup white rice flour

2 tablespoons extra-virgin olive oil

Fine sea salt and freshly ground black pepper

½ cup Chianti, or other full-bodied red wine

1 cup gluten-free chicken broth, plus extra if needed

Pinch hot red pepper flakes

8 large shallots (about 8 ounces), separated along natural divisions

2 tablespoons raisins

2 large garlic cloves, chopped

1 tablespoon tomato paste

2 tablespoons diced pancetta or unsmoked bacon (salt pork)

2 tablespoons brandy

chicken with red and yellow peppers

Simple, fragrant, and colorful—this is what Italian home cooking is all about. Serve this easy dish with Instant Polenta Skillet Bread (page 161) to sop up the good juices.

SERVES 4

3 tablespoons extra-virgin olive oil

1 yellow onion, halved and sliced

1 red bell pepper, trimmed and cut into strips

1 yellow bell pepper, trimmed and cut into strips

4 skinless and boneless chicken thighs, about 1 pound, halved lengthways

2 garlic cloves, sliced

1 cup gluten-free chicken broth

Fine sea salt and freshly ground black pepper

1 tablespoon brine-cured capers, rinsed and drained

2 tablespoons chopped flat-leaf parsley

Warm 2 tablespoons of the olive oil in a large sauté pan over moderate heat. Add the onions and peppers. Sauté until the onions start to soften, about 5 minutes. Cover the pan, lower the heat slightly, and continue cooking until the onions and peppers start to brown, stirring often, about 6 minutes. Transfer to a bowl.

Dust the chicken pieces with the rice flour. Add the remaining tablespoon of olive oil to the pan. Add the chicken and brown on both sides, about 5 minutes. Return the sliced peppers to the pan, and add the garlic. Add the broth, mix well, and season with lightly with salt and pepper.

Partially cover the pan and continue cooking until the chicken and peppers are tender, about 15 minutes. Stir in the capers and parsley and taste for seasoning.

chicken with porcini

Dried Italian porcini mushrooms are expensive but so headily fragrant that you don't need much. They turn everyday chicken into an elegant main course.

Lightly cooked slender green beans and quinoa cooked in chicken broth make good side dishes. (For special occasions, pack the cooked quinoa into a buttered small mold, such as a half-cup measure, and turn out "towers" alongside the chicken and sauce.)

SERVES 4

Soak the porcini in the hot water for 20 minutes. Lift them out, reserving the soaking liquid, and squeeze dry. Chop the porcini and set aside. Strain the aromatic soaking liquid through a paper towel into a small bowl.

Warm 1 tablespoon of the olive oil in a sauté pan over moderate heat. Brown the chicken pieces on both sides, about 7 minutes, in batches if necessary. Transfer to a plate with tongs and season with salt and pepper.

Add the pancetta and onion to the pan and sauté until the onion softens slightly, about 3 minutes. Stir in the chopped porcini and marjoram. Add the strained soaking liquid, scraping with a wooden spoon to loosen any browned bits on the bottom, and bring to a boil. Return the chicken and accumulated juices to the pan and bring to a simmer. Partially cover the pan, and simmer until tender, adding a little of the chicken broth if needed, about 25 minutes.

Meanwhile, warm the remaining tablespoon of olive oil in a skillet over moderate heat. Add the shallots and brown lightly, about 5 minutes. Stir in the mushrooms and sauté until lightly browned, about 2 minutes. Add 2 tablespoons chicken broth. Reduce the heat to low, cover the pan, and cook until tender, about 10 minutes. Check often and stir to make sure that the shallots caramelize but don't scorch.

Add the shallot mixture to the chicken. Taste for seasoning. Stir in the cornstarch mixture and let the sauce bubble until it's clear, glossy, and thickened, 20 seconds or less. (If it becomes too thick, add a little chicken broth; there should be about 1 cup of sauce.)

Scatter the parsley on top. Serve with quinoa.

½ ounce dried porcini

1 cup hot water

2 tablespoons extra-virgin olive oil

4 skinless and boneless chicken thighs, about 1 pound, halved lengthways

Fine sea salt and freshly ground black pepper

4 tablespoons chopped pancetta or unsmoked bacon (salt pork)

1 small yellow onion, finely chopped

½ teaspoon dried marjoram

½ cup gluten-free chicken broth, approximately

¼ pound large shallots, separated along the natural divisions

¼ pound small brown or white mushrooms, halved

2 teaspoons cornstarch mixed with 2 tablespoons water

2 tablespoons chopped flat-leaf parsley

Hot cooked quinoa

braised chicken with green olives and potatoes

You can use almost any variety of large, brine-cured green olive here. The large, mild but flavorful Sicilian type is especially good. However, if the only green olives you can find are small and rather sharp-tasting, such as cocktail olives stuffed with pimiento, blanch them in boiling water for 30 seconds before chopping. It's fine to incorporate the pimiento, too.

SERVES 4

4 skinless and boneless chicken thighs, about 1 pound, halved lengthways

2 tablespoons white rice flour

2 tablespoons extra-virgin olive oil

Fine sea salt and freshly ground black pepper

½ cup dry white wine

2 garlic cloves, chopped

1 teaspoon minced rosemary leaves

½ cup gluten-free chicken broth, plus extra if needed

½ cup pitted and roughly chopped large green olives

2 tablespoons drained and chopped sun-dried tomatoes in oil

2 tablespoons capers, rinsed and drained

8 to 12 tiny potatoes, such as Yukon Gold or Dutch Yellow, unpeeled

2 tablespoons chopped flat-leaf parsley

Dust the chicken thighs with rice flour, shaking off any excess. Warm the olive oil in a large sauté pan over medium-low heat until it shimmers. Brown the chicken pieces on both sides, about 7 minutes, in two batches if necessary. Transfer the chicken to a plate and season with salt and pepper.

Add the wine to the pan, scraping with a wooden spoon to bring up all the browned bits from the bottom of the pan, and bring to a boil. Return the chicken and accumulated juices to the pan and add the garlic and rosemary.

Add the chicken broth and bring to a boil. Reduce the heat to low, partially cover, and simmer for 15 minutes. Turn the chicken pieces, add the olives and sun-dried tomatoes, and a little more chicken broth if necessary to prevent the chicken from drying out. (There should be approximately 1 cup of sauce at the end of cooking time.) Continue cooking, stirring occasionally, until the chicken is tender and no longer pink inside, about 10 minutes more. Stir in the capers. Taste for seasoning.

Meanwhile, cook the potatoes in boiling, salted water to cover until tender, 15 to 20 minutes. Drain and add to the chicken. Sprinkle with the chopped parsley.

deviled chicken with tomato and eggplant

The devilish connection stems from hot red pepper flakes, which liven up but don't overpower this easy recipe, and is complemented by creamy polenta, steamed rice, or any of the crusty breads in Chapter 9.

SERVES 4

Cut the chicken thighs in half lengthways, or into smaller, more or less even-sized pieces if the thighs are very large.

Heat 2 tablespoons of the olive oil in a large sauté pan over moderate heat. Brown the chicken pieces on both sides, about 7 minutes, in two batches if necessary. Transfer to a plate, season lightly with salt and pepper, and sprinkle with the hot pepper flakes.

Add the remaining tablespoon of olive oil to the pan. Add the eggplant, onion, and garlic and cook, stirring often, until softened but not browned, about 5 minutes.

Return the chicken and any accumulated juices to the pan. Stir in the tomatoes. Add the chicken broth and bring to a boil. Reduce the heat to low, partially cover, and simmer for 15 minutes.

Turn the chicken pieces and add the olives and capers. Continue cooking, stirring occasionally, until the chicken is tender and no longer pink inside, about 10 minutes more. Taste for seasoning. Stir in the cornstarch mixture and let the sauce bubble until it thickens and clears, 30 seconds or less. (If the glossy sauce becomes too thick, incorporate a little more chicken broth.)

Divide among four heated dinner plates and sprinkle with the chopped parsley.

1 pound chicken thighs, skinless and boneless

3 tablespoons extra-virgin olive oil

Fine sea salt and freshly ground black pepper

¼ teaspoon hot red pepper flakes, or more to taste

2 small globe eggplants or 1 long Japanese eggplant (6 to 8 ounces), unpeeled, cut in 1-inch chunks

1 medium yellow onion, halved and sliced

2 garlic cloves, sliced

2 large tomatoes or 1 cup canned plum tomatoes, chopped, with juice

¾ cup gluten-free chicken broth, plus extra if needed

12 oil-cured black olives, halved and pitted

1 tablespoon capers, rinsed and drained

2 teaspoons cornstarch dissolved in 2 tablespoons water

2 tablespoons chopped flat-leaf parsley

game hens
with quinoa and pine nut dressing

Even people who claim they dislike quinoa ask for seconds when it's cooked this way. Cutting out the backbone and roasting the birds flat means they not only cook faster, but the breast and leg meat cook evenly and stay juicy. Both the quinoa and the birds can be prepared ahead of time and refrigerated, but bring the hens to room temperature before roasting. This recipe is easy to double.

SERVES 4

QUINOA DRESSING

1 cup quinoa, rinsed (see page 89 for notes about cooking quinoa)

1 tablespoon extra-virgin olive oil, plus extra for baking dish

1 large onion, finely chopped

1 mild Italian pork sausage, 3 to 4 ounces, casing discarded, chopped

1 garlic clove, chopped

2 teaspoons fresh marjoram, or 1 teaspoon dried

½ teaspoon anise seeds

¾ teaspoon fine sea salt

Freshly ground black pepper

1 tart apple (about 6 ounces) such as Granny Smith, peeled, cored, and cut in ½-inch chunks

½ cup raisins

¼ cup pine nuts

Preheat the oven to 350°F.

Bring a large pot of salted water to a boil, add the quinoa, and cook uncovered until tender and the white germ rings show, 8 to 10 minutes. Drain well, spread out on a baking sheet, and let cool.

Preheat the oven to 425°F. Grease an 8 x 10 x 2-inch shallow baking dish with olive oil.

Warm the olive oil over moderate heat in a large skillet. Add the onion and crumbled sausage and cook, stirring often, until the onion is softened and the sausage is cooked through, about 7 minutes. Stir in the garlic, marjoram, anise seeds, salt, a generous grinding of pepper, the apple, raisins, pine nuts, and quinoa. Mix well, and spoon into the baking dish.

Cut the backbone out of each hen using poultry shears or large scissors or by inserting a heavy knife inside the cavity and pressing down hard on either side of the backbone (the attached rib bones are very soft). Rinse the birds and pat dry with paper towels. Season the undersides of the birds with salt and pepper.

Spray a roasting pan lightly with olive oil. Lay the hens in it, skin side up. Fold the wing tips back and tuck under the birds. Rub the surface of the hens with the butter and season with salt and pepper.

Stuffed Zucchini Boats, page 26

Penne and Beans with Pork Ragù, page 69

Chicken Breast Skewers with Quinoa Risotto, page 107

Tortino with Eggs and Cheese, page 92

Fettuccini with Eggplant and Peppers alla Norma, page 58

Oxtail with Pine Nuts and Raisins over
Creamy Polenta, page 153

Tortoni (Amaretti Ice Cream Cake), page 191

Cover the dish of dressing with aluminum foil. Place the hens and dressing in the oven. Roast the hens until tender, basting twice with the pan juices, about 35 minutes. (Juices from a thigh portion should no longer run pink if pierced with a knife tip.)

Remove the foil from the dish of dressing and continue baking until it browns slightly on top, another 10 minutes. Meanwhile, transfer the hens to a heated platter, tent lightly with foil, and let stand for 10 minutes.

TO SERVE: Divide the arugula among four warmed dinner plates. Top with the hen halves and either spoon the dressing alongside or pass it at the table.

GAME HENS

2 Cornish game hens, about 1½ pounds each, preferably organic

Fine sea salt and freshly ground black pepper

Olive oil spray

1 tablespoon unsalted butter, softened

4 handfuls baby arugula or watercress

WHAT IS A CORNISH GAME HEN?

DESPITE THE NAME, it's not a wild game bird and not necessarily female, but a cross between an English breed of chicken from Cornwall and a Plymouth Rock chicken. Very meaty for its bantam size, this American breed was first created in the 1960s. An FDA ruling states that Cornish game hens must not exceed 2 pounds in market weight and be less than 6 weeks old, so you can rest assured that the meat of a game hen (which can be either male or female) is both young and tender. If you're using frozen hens, it's best to thaw them overnight in the refrigerator and bring to room temperature before roasting.

game hens with balsamic onion relish

To prepare this contemporary main course, flattened-out game hens are flavored under the skin with a sage stuffing and roasted until a crispy golden-brown. Both the birds and the sweet-sour onion relish can be prepared ahead of time, even the day before, so it's an easy dish to orchestrate for guests. (If you refrigerate the stuffed hens, bring them to room temperature before roasting.)

SERVES 6

GAME HENS

3 game hens, about 1½ pounds each, preferably organic

Fine sea salt and freshly ground black pepper

8 tablespoons unsalted butter, softened

4 teaspoons crumbled dried sage leaves

1 cup Homemade Bread Crumbs (page 163)

3 ounces (about ¾ cup) grated Parmigiano-Reggiano

2 garlic cloves, crushed and minced

Preheat the oven to 400°F. Have ready a large, rimmed baking sheet lined with aluminum foil.

Cut the backbone out of each hen using poultry shears or large scissors or by inserting a heavy knife inside the cavity and pressing down hard on either side of the backbone. Rinse the birds and pat dry with paper towels. Season the undersides with salt and pepper.

Place all but 1 tablespoon of the butter in a small bowl. Add the sage, bread crumbs, grated Parmesan, and garlic. Season with salt and pepper and mix well.

Lay the hens on the baking sheet, skin side up. Fold the wing tips back and tuck under the birds. Gently loosen the skin over the breast and legs with your fingers and insert in each hen ⅓ of the stuffing, a little at a time. Try to cover as much of the breast and leg meat as possible. Rub the skin of the hens with the remaining tablespoon of butter. Roast until tender, basting twice with the pan juices, about 40 minutes. Juices from a thigh portion should no longer run pink if pierced with a knife tip.

Transfer the hens to a warmed platter, tent lightly with aluminum foil, and let rest for 5 or 10 minutes. Cut each hen in half lengthways, through the breast.

Relish: Warm the olive oil and butter in a heavy saucepan over moderate heat. Add the onions and cook until softened, stirring often, about 10 minutes, reducing the heat as needed. Season lightly with salt and pepper and sprinkle with the sugar. Cook until the onions start to turn golden and caramelize, about 10 minutes more. Add the wine and vinegar and cook until the liquid has almost evaporated, about 2 minutes. Serve warm, or reheat.

To serve: Divide the watercress among six warmed dinner plates, placing it in the center. Top with the hen halves and garnish with the relish.

RELISH

1 tablespoon extra-virgin olive oil

2 tablespoons unsalted butter

3 yellow onions (4 ounces each), halved and thinly sliced

Fine sea salt and freshly ground black pepper

3 teaspoons sugar

3 tablespoons dry white wine

2 tablespoons balsamic vinegar

1 large bunch watercress, large stems removed, rinsed and dried

roast turkey breast florentine

Here's a way to turn inexpensive turkey breast into an elegant roast that serves up to six, depending on the rest of the menu. A side dish of caramelized grape tomatoes (see Caramelized Grape Tomato Crostini, page 171) makes an especially complementary match.

SERVES 4 TO 6

1 turkey half-breast (about 2¼ pounds), with skin and bone

SPINACH STUFFING

2 tablespoons extra-virgin olive oil

1 small onion, finely chopped

4 ounces (about 2 cups) frozen loose-pack spinach

1 garlic clove, chopped

1 large egg

½ cup Homemade Bread Crumbs (page 163)

1 ounce (about ¼ cup) grated Parmigiano-Reggiano

2 tablespoons raw (not roasted and salted) pistachios

1 teaspoon chopped fresh marjoram, or ½ teaspoon dried

Fine sea salt and freshly ground black pepper

Preheat the oven to 400°F.

Place the turkey breast skin side down on a work surface, with the half-attached fillet toward you. Slide a sharp knife blade under the breast bone. Scrape along it and under the rib section to free the bone from the meat and discard the bone. Locate and cut out the tough white tendon from the fillet. "Unfold" the fillet toward you, to get it out of the way, and cut a horizontal pocket into the length of the breast meat, but without cutting all the way through.

Warm 1 tablespoon of the olive oil in a skillet over moderate heat. Add the onion and cook until softened but not browned, about 3 minutes. Stir in the spinach and garlic, cover the pan, reduce the heat to low, and steam until the spinach has thawed and softened, about 4 minutes. Check occasionally to make sure it is not sticking.

Crack the egg into a bowl, beat lightly, and stir in the bread crumbs, Parmesan, pistachios, marjoram, about ¼ teaspoon salt, a generous grinding of black pepper, and the spinach mixture.

Insert as much of the stuffing as will fit in the pocket of the turkey breast, probably more than half of the total. Replace the flap of fillet, covering the stuffing. Starting at the center, tie the roast at 1-inch intervals with butcher's twine. Make a final loop lengthways, to secure both ends, and once around (like tying a gift box ribbon). Reserve the remaining stuffing.

Lay a 12 x 14-inch sheet of foil on a work surface. Center the tied roast on the foil skin side up. Season lightly with salt and pepper. Fold up the sides of the foil, making several layers, to form a snug container with 1-inch high sides. Smear the top and sides of the roast with the butter, to promote browning. Roast until an instant-read meat thermometer inserted at an angle reaches 160°–165°F, about 45 minutes. Transfer the roast to a warmed platter, tent it loosely with foil, and let rest for 10 minutes. The internal temperature will continue to rise slightly.

Meanwhile, warm the remaining tablespoon of olive oil in the skillet over medium-low heat. Form the leftover spinach stuffing into 1-inch balls and dredge lightly in the rice flour. Flatten them slightly into patties and fry until golden brown on both sides, about 3 minutes total.

Lift the turkey roll from its improvised foil container, reserving the juices, and place on a cutting board.

To make a light sauce, combine the turkey juices with an equal amount of chicken broth in a small saucepan and bring to a simmer.

Carve the turkey roll into ½-inch thick slices. Divide among warmed plates and drizzle with the sauce. Garnish with the spinach patties.

TIP: These miniature spinach patties are so popular that it's worth making up a batch of stuffing, without the turkey, and serving them often as an appetizer.

2 teaspoons unsalted butter

¼ cup white rice flour, for dredging the stuffing patties

½ cup gluten-free chicken broth, approximately

turkey and sausage meatballs with chunky tomato sauce

The addition of bread crumbs makes all the difference to Italian meatballs—polpette—as they absorb and retain the good juices. Make the fresh-tasting, colorful sauce first and let it simmer while you cook the meatballs.

SERVES 2

CHUNKY TOMATO SAUCE

1 tablespoon extra-virgin olive oil

1 yellow onion, finely chopped

1 medium carrot, grated

1 garlic clove, chopped

¼ teaspoon celery seeds, slightly crushed

1 (14- to 15-ounce) can Italian plum tomatoes, roughly chopped, juice included

Fine sea salt and freshly ground black pepper

MEATBALLS

1 large egg

¼ cup Homemade Bread Crumbs (page 163), or 2 tablespoons quinoa flakes

4 sage leaves, chopped, or ½ teaspoon dried sage

3 tablespoons grated Parmigiano-Reggiano

¼ teaspoon fine sea salt

Freshly ground black pepper

½ pound ground turkey thigh meat

1 mild Italian sausage, 3 to 4 ounces, casing removed

¼ cup white rice flour

1 tablespoon extra-virgin olive oil

2 tablespoons chopped flat-leaf parsley

SAUCE: Warm the olive oil in a heavy saucepan over medium-low heat. Add the onion, carrot, garlic, and celery seeds and cook, stirring often, until softened, about 5 minutes. Add the tomatoes, season with salt and pepper, and bring to a boil. Reduce the heat to low and simmer, stirring often, until slightly reduced and tender but still chunky, about 30 minutes.

MEATBALLS: Crack the egg into a bowl and beat lightly. Add the bread crumbs, sage, Parmesan, salt, and a generous grinding of pepper and mix well. Crumble the ground turkey and the sausage meat into the mixture and stir together until evenly combined. Moisten your hands with water and form walnut-size balls. Roll in the rice flour.

In a skillet large enough to hold the meatballs without crowding, warm the olive oil over moderate heat. Add the meatballs. Brown on all sides, turning them often and shaking the pan occasionally to prevent sticking, about 7 minutes.

Divide the meatballs between serving plates and top with a band of sauce, but don't mask them completely. Sprinkle with the parsley.

catch of the day

AS WITH ANY country blessed with a long coastline and ancient fishing traditions, great Italian fish dishes are legion. And, of course, dependent on the impeccably fresh local catch. Everything edible that swims in the sea finds its way to the table, from sardines to huge tuna, and inland lakes and waterways yield freshwater fish that doesn't go unappreciated.

With practicality in mind, I've included fish and seafood recipes in the Italian style that make full use of frozen fish and seafood, but by all means use fresh fish if you can find it. (Just make sure that it was delivered fresh, or thawed, that day.)

While fishing for recipe ideas, don't overlook the fabulous Italian-American fish soup-stew Cioppino (page 52, in the soup chapter), which is always a huge success for a casual gathering; the company-worthy Baked Shrimp with garlicky gluten-free bread crumbs (page 134); or one of my quick weeknight favorites Baked Cod with Parsley and Green Onions (page 131).

halibut with fresh tomato sauce

Fresh, flavorful, and easy to cook, this is an ideal dish for summer. The smooth, brilliantly colored sauce, which is served at room temperature, contains both olive oil and vinegar, so there's no need to dress the baby greens.

SERVES 4

Preheat the oven to 425°F. Set out a shallow baking dish large enough to hold the halibut filets in one layer with a little space between them and grease with butter.

Arrange the fish in the baking dish. Sprinkle with the salt, pepper, lemon juice, and dill. Dot with the cubed butter. Bake until the fish is cooked through and flakes easily, 12 to 15 minutes.

Meanwhile, make the sauce. Cut a cross in the base of each tomato and cover with boiling water. Let stand for 10 seconds and drain. When cool enough to handle, pull off the skins. Cut each tomato in half and squeeze gently (over the sink) to expel the seeds. Chop and transfer to a food processor. Add the vinegar and olive oil, and season lightly with salt and pepper, and blend until smooth. Taste for seasoning, adding salt or pepper as needed. Depending on the sweetness of the tomatoes (really good ones won't need it), add a pinch of sugar to balance the vinegar. Add the capers and transfer to a bowl.

Preheat a ridged grill pan or heavy skillet. Spray both sides of the bread slices with olive oil and grill or fry until lightly browned, turning once.

TO SERVE: Center a handful of baby greens on each plate. Place the halibut on top and drizzle it with any buttery juices in the baking dish. Spoon some of the tomato sauce over each serving. Pass the rest in a small glass bowl (to show off the color) at the table. Garnish each serving with the grilled crostini.

3 tablespoons unsalted butter, cut in small cubes, plus more for baking dish

4 halibut fillets, about 6 ounces each

Fine sea salt and freshly ground black pepper

Juice of 1 lemon

1 tablespoon chopped fresh dill or tarragon

FRESH TOMATO SAUCE

2 pounds vine-ripened tomatoes, preferably sweet heirloom variety

4 tablespoons red wine vinegar

3/4 cup extra-virgin olive oil

Fine sea salt and freshly ground black pepper

Pinch sugar, optional

2 tablespoons bottled capers, drained and rinsed

8 to 12 diagonal slices of Italian-Style Baguette (page 158)

Olive oil spray

4 handfuls mixed baby salad greens

baked swordfish
with potatoes, sicilian style

Swordfish's mild flavor and meaty texture contrast nicely with three Sicilian staples: anchovies, olives, and tomatoes. All these good flavors are absorbed by waxy-type potatoes, which don't fall apart as they cook, to make a satisfying main course.

SERVES 4

4 swordfish steaks, about 6 ounces each, 3/4-inch thick

4 canned anchovy fillets, drained and chopped

1 teaspoon grated lemon zest

4 tablespoons extra-virgin olive oil

Freshly ground black pepper

1½ pounds medium waxy-type potatoes, such as Yukon Gold or Dutch Yellow, unpeeled

2 medium onions, halved and sliced

½ cup oil-cured black olives, pitted and quartered

2 cups peeled and chopped ripe tomatoes (or boxed Italian Pomi brand chopped tomatoes)

Fine sea salt

3 tablespoons gluten-free Homemade Bread Crumbs (page 163)

Olive oil spray

2 tablespoons chopped flat-leaf parsley

Pat the swordfish steaks dry and place on a plate. Mash the anchovies to a paste with the lemon zest and 2 tablespoons of the olive oil. Add a generous grinding of black pepper, and spread this paste over the fish.

Boil the potatoes until tender, about 20 minutes. When cool enough to handle, peel and slice thinly.

Meanwhile, warm the remaining 2 tablespoons of olive oil in a large skillet over moderate heat. Add the onion and cook, stirring often, until light gold and tender, about 10 minutes. Stir in the olives and tomatoes. Simmer for a further 10 minutes, until slightly thickened.

Preheat the oven to 425°F. Spoon half the sauce into a baking dish large enough to hold the fish in one layer. Arrange the swordfish on top. Top each portion with an overlapping layer of potatoes, and stand the remaining slices upright around the edge of the dish. Season lightly with salt and pepper. Cover with the remaining tomato sauce. Sprinkle the steaks with the bread crumbs and spray with olive oil.

Bake until the sauce bubbles and the fish is cooked through and opaque in the middle (check with a knife tip), about 15 minutes. Top with the parsley.

red snapper and tomato gratinato

This easy, appetizing supper dish would not be out of place on the menu of any popular neighborhood trattoria. You can substitute other firm white fish fillets for equally good results.

SERVES 4

Preheat the oven to 350°F. Spray a shallow baking dish large enough to hold the fish fillets in one layer with olive oil.

Lightly toast the bread crumbs in an ungreased heavy skillet over medium-low heat, about 2 minutes, and set aside.

Warm the olive oil in a skillet over moderate heat. Sauté the zucchini until softened and starting to brown, about 5 minutes. Stir in the garlic, continue cooking for 1 minute, and remove from the heat. Season with salt and pepper.

Lay the fish fillets in the baking dish and sprinkle with the fennel seeds. Season lightly with salt and pepper. Top with the capers, zucchini, and chopped tomatoes. Sprinkle the bread crumbs on top, and spray with olive oil.

Bake until the fish is cooked through and flakes easily, about 20 minutes.

Olive oil spray

½ cup gluten-free Homemade Bread Crumbs (page 163)

2 tablespoons extra-virgin olive oil

2 medium zucchini, cut in small dice

2 garlic cloves, chopped

Fine sea salt and freshly ground black pepper

1¼ to 1½ pounds red snapper fillets

¼ teaspoon fennel seeds, lightly crushed

2 teaspoons capers, rinsed and drained

2 cups peeled and chopped ripe tomatoes (or boxed Italian Pomi brand chopped tomatoes)

tuna salad with green beans, potatoes, and olives

A quintessentially Mediterranean main course salad, this one shares several ingredients with French Salad Niçoise but has its own personality. For optimal flavor and texture, have all the components freshly cooked and cooled, but not refrigerated.

SERVES 4

4 large eggs

6 tablespoons extra-virgin olive oil

2 tablespoons red wine vinegar

Fine sea salt and freshly ground black pepper

1 pound tiny, waxy-type potatoes, such as Yukon Gold or Dutch Yellow, unpeeled

1 pound tiny French green beans, topped but not tailed

2 tablespoons capers, rinsed and drained

2 tablespoons thinly sliced oil-packed, sun-dried tomatoes

2 (6-ounce) cans wild-caught Mediterranean tuna in olive oil, such as Genoa brand

20 oil-cured black olives, halved and pitted

Italian-Style Baguette (page 158), freshly baked or frozen and reheated

Place the eggs in a pan with enough cold water to cover by ½ inch. Bring to a rolling boil. Cover the pan, remove from the heat, and let stand for 12 minutes.

Drain the eggs (they will be perfectly hard boiled) and let cool. When ready to serve, shell the eggs, cut in quarters and sprinkle with a little salt.

Whisk the olive oil and vinegar together and season to taste with salt and pepper.

Cook the potatoes in their skins in boiling, salted water until tender, about 20 minutes. Remove the potatoes with a slotted spoon to a bowl. Add the beans to the same cooking water and cook until barely tender, about 2 minutes. Drain the beans and place them in a separate bowl. Pour half the olive oil and vinegar dressing over the warm beans and toss to mix. Toss the warm potatoes, capers, and sun-dried tomatoes with the other half of the dressing. Let cool to room temperature.

Arrange bands of beans and potatoes in a large, shallow serving dish, preferably rectangular. Top with the tuna, separated into chunks, olives, and wedges of egg.

Serve with the bread.

tuna salad with white beans

Just right for lunch in warm weather, this Mediterranean salad can be put together in a few minutes. Be sure to use tuna canned in olive oil for its superior texture and flavor.

SERVES 2

Tip the beans into a serving bowl, liquid and all. Sprinkle with the vinegar and add a generous grinding of black pepper. Add the tomatoes and olives and stir gently to mix. Top with the tuna, breaking it up slightly into large chunks, and drizzle with the flavorful olive oil left in the can.

Preheat a ridged grill pan or heavy skillet. Spray both sides of the bread slices with olive oil and grill or fry until lightly browned, turning once. Rub one side of the crostini with the cut sides of the garlic, and serve with the tuna salad.

1 (15-ounce) can white kidney beans (cannellini)

1 tablespoon white wine vinegar

Freshly ground black pepper

1 cup mixed red and yellow baby tomatoes

6 oil-cured black olives, halved and pitted

1 (6-ounce) can Mediterranean tuna in olive oil, such as Genoa brand, oil included

8 diagonal slices of Italian-Style Baguette (page 158)

Olive oil spray

1 large garlic clove, halved

pan-fried fillets of sole

White rice flour makes an outstanding "breading" for pan-fried fish as it promotes a nice, crisp surface. Have everything ready, including heated serving plates, before you start. It's an ephemeral sort of dish; you need to cook it fast to make it perfect. And using impeccably fresh fish is a must for this classic dish—be sure it was delivered that day. Boiled tiny potatoes and lightly cooked broccoli or asparagus make suitable side dishes.

SERVES 2

3 tablespoons white rice flour

Fine sea salt and freshly ground black pepper

2 fresh sole fillets, 6 to 8 ounces each

2 tablespoons extra-virgin olive oil

3 tablespoons unsalted butter

4 tablespoons lemon juice

2 teaspoons capers, rinsed and drained

2 tablespoons chopped flat-leaf parsley

Lemon wedges

Put the rice flour on a plate, sprinkle with salt and pepper, and mix well. Coat the fish on both sides, shaking off any excess.

Warm the olive oil with 1 tablespoon of the butter in a large skillet over moderate heat. Add the fish fillets and fry for about 2 minutes on each side, until light gold and cooked through. Using a slotted spatula, transfer to heated plates.

Take the pan off the heat and add the lemon juice (it will hiss) and the remaining 2 tablespoons of butter. Return the pan to the heat and stir until the butter starts to turn golden brown and smells nutty, about 30 seconds. Remove from the heat and stir in the capers. Pour over the fish, and season lightly with salt and pepper.

Sprinkle with the parsley, and garnish with lemon wedges.

baked cod with parsley and green onions

This dish might sound unassuming, but don't pass it by—it's delicious. Any firm white fish fillets can be cooked this way. Italian cooks use whatever fresh white fish fillets come to hand and call the result gratinato verde, or green gratin. Don't stint on the olive oil here. A quick first course of Off-the-Shelf White Bean, Sage, and Pumpkin Soup (page 50) completes the meal nicely, along with grilled gluten-free bread from your freezer.

SERVES 2

Preheat the oven to 425°F. Using 1 tablespoon of the olive oil, grease a shallow baking dish large enough to hold the fish fillets in one layer.

Lay the fish in the baking dish and season with salt and pepper. Sprinkle with the green onions, parsley, and capers and top with the bread crumbs. Drizzle with the remaining 3 tablespoons olive oil. Bake until the fish is just cooked through and the crumbs are starting to brown, 12 to 15 minutes. Serve garnished with lemon wedges.

4 tablespoons extra-virgin olive oil

¾ to 1 pound fresh cod fillets

Fine sea salt and freshly ground black pepper

3 tablespoons finely chopped green onions

2 tablespoons chopped flat-leaf parsley

1 teaspoon capers, drained and rinsed

4 tablespoons Homemade Bread Crumbs (page 163)

Lemon wedges

trout with pine nuts and capers

Lemon and capers provide a tangy flavor contrast for the delicate flesh of trout. If you double the recipe, cook two fish at a time (wiping out the pan with paper towels between batches) and keep the first two warm in a low oven. Small, smooth-skinned potatoes, boiled in their skins, always go well with trout. Fingerlings, Dutch Baby Yellow, and Yukon Gold are all good.

SERVES 2

2 boned trout, 6 to 8 ounces each

Fine sea salt and freshly ground black pepper

2 tablespoons white rice flour

2 tablespoons extra-virgin olive oil

2 tablespoons unsalted butter

2 tablespoons pine nuts

1 tablespoon capers, rinsed and drained

Lemon wedges

Rinse the trout and pat dry with paper towels. Cut off the heads, fins, and tails.

Season the insides with salt and pepper. Roll the trout in the flour, shaking off any surplus.

In a pan just large enough to hold the trout easily, warm the olive oil over moderate heat. Add the fish and cook on both sides until the skin is golden-brown and crispy, about 3 minutes per side, reducing the heat slightly as needed. Season with salt and pepper. Transfer to warmed plates.

Meanwhile, melt the butter in a small pan over medium-low heat. Add the pine nuts and sauté until they and the butter turn golden, 1 minute or less. Remove from the heat and add the capers.

Spoon the sauce over the cooked trout and serve with lemon wedges for squeezing over the fish.

trout with rosemary and almonds

A hint of rosemary complements trout nicely, and sliced almonds offer a crunchy contrast. You can double the recipe, but cook two fish at a time (wiping out the pan with paper towels between batches) and keep the first two warm in a low oven. Serve with tiny potatoes boiled in their skins.

SERVES 2

Rinse the trout and pat dry with paper towels. Cut off the heads, fins, and tails.

Season the insides with salt and pepper. Roll the trout in the flour, shaking off any surplus. Tuck the rosemary inside the cavities.

In a pan just large enough to hold the trout easily, warm the olive oil and 2 tablespoons of the butter over moderate heat. Add the fish and cook on both sides until the skin is golden-brown and crispy, about 3 minutes per side, reducing the heat slightly as needed. Season with salt and pepper. Add the almonds around the edges of the pan during the last minute of cooking, turning them often to make sure they don't get too brown.

After removing the fish to warmed plates, melt the remaining tablespoon of butter in the pan, and pour the almonds and lightly browned butter over the trout.

2 boned trout, 6 to 8 ounces each

Fine sea salt and freshly ground black pepper

2 tablespoons white rice flour

4 small rosemary sprigs

2 tablespoons extra-virgin olive oil

3 tablespoons unsalted butter

2 tablespoons sliced almonds

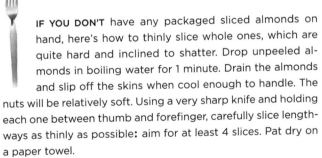

SLICING ALMONDS

IF YOU DON'T have any packaged sliced almonds on hand, here's how to thinly slice whole ones, which are quite hard and inclined to shatter. Drop unpeeled almonds in boiling water for 1 minute. Drain the almonds and slip off the skins when cool enough to handle. The nuts will be relatively soft. Using a very sharp knife and holding each one between thumb and forefinger, carefully slice lengthways as thinly as possible: aim for at least 4 slices. Pat dry on a paper towel.

baked shrimp with garlic bread crumbs

Serve these flavorful shrimp with Italian-Style Baguettes (page 158) to mop up the good juices and a generous supply of paper napkins. If fresh shrimp are not an option, use a 1-pound bag of large frozen shrimp and thaw according to the package directions.

SERVES 4

1½ pounds jumbo shrimp, shelled and deveined, tails left on

6 tablespoons extra-virgin olive oil

Juice of ½ lemon

2 large garlic cloves, 1 finely chopped and 1 cut in half

Small handful of basil leaves, torn up

2 tablespoons finely chopped flat-leaf parsley

½ teaspoon fine sea salt, plus more as needed

Freshly ground black pepper

½ cup Homemade Bread Crumbs (page 163)

Arrange the shrimp in a shallow baking dish large enough to hold them in one layer. Top with 5 tablespoons of the olive oil, lemon juice, chopped garlic, basil, parsley, salt, and a generous grinding of pepper. Turn the shrimp over to coat well, cover the dish with plastic wrap, and let stand at room temperature for 20 minutes.

Meanwhile, warm the remaining tablespoon of olive oil in a small skillet over moderate heat. Add the halved garlic and cook until golden, about 1 minute. Discard the garlic and add the bread crumbs. Remove from the heat and stir to coat with oil. Season lightly with salt and pepper.

Preheat the oven to 400°F. Sprinkle the bread crumbs over the shrimp. Bake until pink and cooked through, about 10 minutes.

pork, lamb, and beef

ALL FRESH MEATS are gluten-free, but not all the offerings at the meat counter are created equal. If possible, opt for cuts of meat that come from humanely raised, well cared-for animals. This not only keeps heritage breeds alive and well, not to mention beleaguered family farmers, but the end result has true flavor and texture.

Italian veal recipes are legion—Italy doesn't have a lot of flat pastureland for grazing cattle—but free-raised veal is in short supply in the United States. Pork fillets from humanely raised pigs make a readily available "white meat" alternative that works beautifully.

I haven't included recipes for classics like Florentine-style steaks or garlic-studded leg of lamb because as they don't involve gluten, they don't present a problem. Instead, I re-worked (and often lightened) mouthwatering Italian meat dishes that would otherwise be off-limits for the gluten-intolerant. Enjoy!

pork scaloppine with mushrooms and marsala

Tender little pork scaloppine, cut from the fillet, cook in less than 5 minutes and get topped with a quick mushroom pan sauce. It's simple but tastes luxurious.

SERVES 4

Shave off any fat or silvery skin from the pork fillet with a sharp knife. Cut on the diagonal into ½-inch thick slices. (Freeze the ends of the fillet for another use.) Place the slices between sheets of plastic wrap and pound lightly to ¼-inch thick. Dip in the rice flour, shaking off any excess.

Warm the olive oil and 2 tablespoons of the butter in a large skillet over moderate heat. Working in batches, cook the pork slices on both sides until barely cooked through and starting to brown, about 2 minutes on each side. Remove to a platter, season with salt and pepper, and keep warm.

Add the mushrooms to the pan and sauté until glassy-looking and tender, about 3 minutes. Stir in the Marsala and cook, stirring up any browned bits from the bottom with a wooden spoon until slightly reduced, about 30 seconds.

Return the pork slices to the pan, turn over in the sauce, and heat through, about 30 seconds. Overlap the scaloppine on heated dinner plates. Stir the remaining tablespoon of butter into the sauce and spoon over the pork. Sprinkle with the parsley.

1 large pork fillet, about 1¼ pounds

¼ cup white rice flour

1 tablespoon extra-virgin olive oil

3 tablespoons unsalted butter

Fine sea salt and freshly ground black pepper

12 medium white mushrooms, sliced

⅓ cup dry Marsala

2 tablespoons chopped flat-leaf parsley

pork fillet rolls with red wine sauce

All over Italy, Italian cooks wrap small squares of veal around a savory stuffing to make rollatini (little rolls) for frying or grilling. Pounded slices of readily available American pork fillet works well instead.

SERVES 4

STUFFING

½ cup Homemade Bread Crumbs (page 163)

1 ounce shredded Fontina or Gruyère

2 tablespoons grated Parmigiano-Reggiano

2 tablespoons thinly sliced and finely chopped salame

1 tablespoon chopped flat-leaf parsley

¼ teaspoon dried sage

1 tablespoon minced green onion

1 teaspoon minced lemon zest

¼ teaspoon fine sea salt

Freshly ground black pepper

1 tablespoon extra-virgin olive oil

1 large egg yolk

1 large pork fillet, 1¼ pounds

2 tablespoons extra-virgin olive oil

⅓ cup dry red wine, such as Chianti

⅓ cup gluten-free beef broth

1 tablespoon butter

In a large bowl, combine the bread crumbs, Fontina, Parmesan, salame, parsley, sage, green onion, and lemon zest. Add salt and a generous grinding of black pepper. Stir in the olive oil and egg yolk. The stuffing should be slightly moist; add a few more bread crumbs if it's too wet or a little more olive oil if it's too dry.

Remove any fat or silvery skin from the pork fillets and cut on the diagonal into twelve even slices, ½ inch thick. Place between sheets of plastic wrap and pound into 3 x 4-inch rectangles.

Place a scant tablespoon of filling on the bottom third of each. Roll the pork around the filling into a tight log, tucking in the sides as you go. Pin with a toothpick inserted lengthways. (Rolls can be assembled to this point and refrigerated overnight, but bring to room temperature before cooking.)

Warm the olive oil in a large sauté pan over moderate heat. Brown the pork rolls on all sides, about 6 minutes. Transfer to a heated plate and keep warm.

Pour off all but a film of oil, and deglaze the pan with the wine, scraping up any stuck brown bits. Let evaporate by one third and add the beef broth. Let it bubble until the liquid is slightly reduced and syrupy, then stir in the butter. Divide the pork rolls among heated plates and top with the sauce.

sliced pork fillet with caramelized onions and fontina

Crispy gluten-free bread crumbs provide the finishing touch on this combination of tender pork, onions, and melted cheese. If you don't have any individual gratin dishes, use one large shallow baking dish instead, but group each portion separately in the dish for easy serving.

SERVES 4

Shave off any fat or silvery skin from the pork fillet. Cut diagonally into sixteen ½-inch thick slices. (Freeze the ends of the fillet for another use; you want perfectly even slices for this dish so they cook in the same length of time.)

Warm 2 tablespoons of the butter and the olive oil in a large, heavy skillet over moderate heat. Brown the pork slices on both sides, about 3 minutes. The pork should be just cooked, but remain faintly pink in the center. It will finish cooking later. Remove with a slotted spoon and divide among four 7-inch diameter gratin dishes. Season lightly with salt and pepper.

Melt the remaining 2 tablespoons of butter in the same pan, add the onions, and season lightly with salt and pepper. Sauté over moderate heat until tender and golden-brown, about 8 minutes. Spoon over the pork. Remove the pan from the heat, add the bread crumbs, and stir to coat with butter.

Heat the broiler. Pour 2 tablespoons of the wine into each dish. Top with one quarter of the cheese and one quarter of the bread crumbs. Spray lightly with olive oil. Place the dishes under the heat and broil until the cheese starts to melt and the topping browns, about 2 minutes. Dust with the parsley and serve garnished with the lemon wedges.

2 pork fillets,
12 to 16 ounces each

4 tablespoons
unsalted butter

1 tablespoon
extra-virgin olive oil

Fine sea salt and freshly
ground black pepper

4 medium yellow onions,
halved and thinly sliced

½ cup Homemade Bread
Crumbs (page 163)

½ cup dry white wine,
such as Pinot Grigio

½ cup finely diced
Fontina or shredded
Gruyère

Olive oil spray

2 tablespoons
chopped flat-leaf parsley

4 lemon wedges

pork fillet with prune-apple stuffing and saffron rice

This elegant roast takes just 20 minutes in the oven, is simple to carve, and looks impressive. Vacuum-packed pancetta works well here as the slices are nice and thin but firm and well-shaped. Always remove any silvery skin from the pork fillet, as it toughens when cooked.

SERVES 6

8 soft-pack pitted prunes

1 small crisp apple, such as Gala, peeled, cored, and cut into 8 sections

1 bay leaf

1 cup dry white wine, such as Pinot Grigio

2 pork fillets, 16 ounces each

Fine sea salt and freshly ground black pepper

18 thin slices pancetta or unsmoked bacon (salt pork), about 3 ounces

2 teaspoons extra-virgin olive oil

1½ cups gluten-free chicken broth

2 teaspoons cornstarch dissolved in 2 tablespoons cold water

Saffron Rice (page 142)

Combine the prunes, apple, bay leaf and wine in a saucepan and bring to a boil. Reduce the heat to low and simmer the fruit until tender, about 10 minutes. Lift out the prunes and apple wedges with a slotted spoon (reserve the wine) and let cool.

Shave off any fat or silvery skin from the pork fillets. Butterfly the meat by slicing almost all the way through, then open the meat out like a book and place between sheets of plastic wrap. Pound with a rolling pin to an even thickness of about ½ inch, making two rectangles approximately 5 by 11 inches. Discard the top sheet of plastic wrap, and season the meat lightly with salt and pepper.

Top each flattened fillet with 4 slices of the pancetta, centering them along its length. Alternate 4 prunes and 4 apple sections on top. Using the plastic wrap to help you, roll up lengthways to enclose the filling, tucking in the sides as you go. Place seam side down on a cutting board, discarding the plastic. Top each roll with 5 of the remaining slices of pancetta, partly covering the ends of the rolls with the first and last slice. Tie in place with butcher's twine at 1-inch intervals.

Rub the tied rolls all over with the olive oil and let them stand at room temperature for 30 minutes for the flavors to permeate. (If preparing ahead, refrigerate for up to 24 hours, but bring to room temperature before roasting.)

Preheat the oven to 400°F. Arrange the rolls 3 inches apart in a heavy, ovenproof skillet. Roast until cooked through, about 20 minutes. Transfer to a heated platter, tent it lightly with foil, and let the rolls rest for 10 minutes.

Cover the handle of the hot skillet with a mitt and place it over moderate heat. Add the reserved wine and let it evaporate by half. Add the broth and bring the mixture to a boil, stirring up any brown bits stuck to the pan. Add the cornstarch mixture and stir until the sauce thickens, 30 seconds or less.

TO SERVE: Remove the string from the pork fillets. Carve the meat on the diagonal into ½-inch thick slices and fan out on heated plates. Stir any carving juices into the sauce, and taste for seasoning. Spoon the sauce over the meat and serve the Saffron Rice alongside.

saffron rice

1 cup gluten-free
chicken broth

1 cup water

Pinch fine sea salt

1 tablespoon
unsalted butter

¼ teaspoon saffron
threads

1 cup long-grain
white rice

Combine the broth, water, salt, and butter and bring to a boil.
Add the saffron, crumbling the threads with your fingers. Add
the rice, reduce the heat to low, and simmer until the liquid has
been absorbed and the rice is tender and fluffy, about 17 minutes.

SAFFRON

THE MOST EXPENSIVE of all spices, saffron has been
revered and sought after for thousands of years. Used
by the ancient Romans (the wealthy ones, at any rate)
to flavor foods and wines, as a dye, and for its medicinal
properties, saffron is simply the dried, orange-red,
threadlike stigmas of the saffron crocus, *crocus sativus*. As the
stigmas have to be picked out by hand, and it takes about
20,000 blossoms to produce just four ounces of the precious
dried strands, the high cost of production is understandable.

Fortunately, just a small pinch of saffron will impart its
unique flavor, aroma, and golden color to such classic dishes
as Milanese risotto, Spanish paella, French bouillabaisse,
Swedish Santa Lucia breads and buns, and any number of ex-
otic Middle Eastern and Indian dishes.

Always buy saffron threads, as powdered saffron can be
adulterated with cheap fillers. Inexpensive ground turmeric and
ground safflower (sometimes known as Mexican saffron) will
impart a yellow color, but not the unique flavor of saffron. You'll
find genuine saffron in the spice section of grocery stores like
Whole Foods.

braised pork in white wine with savoy cabbage

Inspired by a rustic dish of pork and cabbage from Lombardy, the succulent meat is served on a bed of buttery, lightly cooked, shredded Savoy cabbage. Serve with polenta or Italian-Style Baguettes (page 158), as the sauce is much too good to leave on the plate.

SERVES 4 TO 6

Warm the olive oil in a large sauté pan over moderate heat. Brown the pork in batches, without crowding the pan, and transfer it to a heavy pot. Season with salt and pepper.

Add the onion, carrot, pancetta, sausage balls, and garlic to the sauté pan. Cook until the onion softens, about 5 minutes, stirring often. Add the wine, and scrape up all the browned bits in the bottom of the pan with a wooden spoon. Pour the mixture over the meat. Add the broth, stir well, and simmer, covered, over low heat until the pork is almost done, about 1 hour.

Add the raisins to the pot and continue cooking until the meat is tender, about 15 minutes more. Stir the cornstarch mixture and add it to the sauce. Let it simmer, stirring, until it clears and thickens slightly, about 20 seconds. Taste, and adjust seasoning if needed.

Shortly before the pork is ready, add the shredded cabbage to boiling, salted water. After it returns to a boil, cook for 2 minutes. Drain in a colander, rinse under cold water, and drain again. Melt the butter in a large skillet over moderate heat. Add the cabbage and sauté until tender, about 2 minutes. Season with salt and pepper.

Arrange a bed of cabbage on each dinner plate. Spoon the pork on top, leaving a band of cabbage showing around the edges.

2 tablespoons extra-virgin olive oil

2 pounds boneless pork shoulder, cut into 1-inch cubes, excess fat discarded

Fine sea salt and freshly ground black pepper

1 medium yellow onion, coarsely chopped

1 large carrot, diced

2 tablespoons chopped pancetta or unsmoked bacon (salt pork)

2 mild Italian pork sausages (3 to 4 ounces each), casings removed and formed into small balls

2 garlic cloves

1 cup dry white wine, such as Pinot Grigio

1 cup gluten-free chicken broth

½ cup yellow raisins

2 teaspoons cornstarch mixed with 2 tablespoons cold water

1 head Savoy (crinkly) cabbage, about 1½ pounds, quartered, cored, and thinly sliced

2 tablespoons unsalted butter

pork fillet with pesto stuffing

Genoa's now world-famous signature pasta sauce, made with aromatic fresh basil leaves, olive oil, garlic, and Parmesan, turns roast pork fillet into an elegant new roast that's wonderfully easy to cook and serve. Enjoy either Fettuccine with Eggplant and Peppers alla Norma (page 58) or Fettuccine with Scallops and Zucchini (page 59) as a complementary, easy first course while the roast rests.

SERVES 6

2 pork fillets, about 1¼ pounds each

Freshly ground black pepper

4 tablespoons Pesto Sauce (page 49), or from a jar

½ cup Homemade Bread Crumbs (page 163)

1 ounce (about ¼ cup) grated Pecorino Romano

1 tablespoon extra-virgin olive oil

2 tablespoons unsalted butter, softened

½ cup dry white wine

1 cup gluten-free chicken broth

Fine sea salt, optional

1 teaspoon cornstarch dissolved in 1 tablespoon cold water

Shave off any fat or silvery skin from the pork fillets. Butterfly the meat by slicing almost all the way through, then open the meat out like a book. Repeat the lengthways cut along the center of each half without cutting all the way through. Place the meat between sheets of plastic wrap. Pound with a rolling pin to an even thickness of about ½ inch, making two rectangles approximately 6 by 12 inches. Discard the top sheet of plastic wrap and season the meat lightly with pepper.

Combine the pesto, bread crumbs, pecorino, and olive oil. Spread each pork rectangle with half the mixture, spreading it to within ½ inch of the edges. Using the plastic wrap to help you, roll each one lengthways to enclose the filling, tucking in the sides as you go. Place seam side down on a cutting board, discarding the plastic wrap. Tie with butcher's twine at 1-inch intervals. Rub each pork roll all over with half the butter. Let stand at room temperature for 30 minutes for the flavors to permeate.

Preheat the oven to 400°F. Heat an ovenproof skillet (preferably cast iron) large enough to hold both fillets. Place the pork rolls in the hot skillet, seam side up, and put it in the oven. Roast until the meat is cooked through but still pinkish in the center (an internal temperature of 150°), about 25 minutes. Transfer the rolls to a heated platter, tent them lightly with foil, and let the rolls rest for 10 minutes. The internal temperature will continue to rise slightly.

Cover the handle of the hot skillet with a mitt and place it over moderate heat. Add the wine and let it reduce slightly. Add the broth and bring the mixture to a boil, stirring up any brown bits stuck to the pan. Taste for seasoning and add salt and pepper if needed. Add the cornstarch mixture and stir until the sauce thickens, 20 seconds or less.

To serve: Remove the string from the pork fillets. Carve the meat on the diagonal into ½-inch thick slices and fan out on heated plates. Stir any carving juices into the sauce, and taste for seasoning. Spoon the sauce over the meat.

pork meatballs and lentils

In this delicious combination that's also high in inexpensive protein, lentils absorb the good flavors of the sauce ingredients but retain their texture. It's a dish that freezes well, so it's a good plan to double the recipe and store half for another night, in which case mix the meatballs in with the lentils.

SERVES 4

LENTILS

3 tablespoon extra-virgin olive oil

1 small onion, finely chopped

1 medium carrot, finely diced

2 tablespoons chopped pancetta or unsmoked bacon (salt pork)

1 (14- to 15-ounce) can Italian plum tomatoes to supply 1 cup tomatoes, juice included (reserve remainder for another use)

1 cup lentils, preferably brown Umbrian lentils or green le Puy lentils, rinsed

2 cups gluten-free chicken broth, plus extra if needed

Fine sea salt and freshly ground black pepper

PORK MEATBALLS

3 canned anchovy fillets

1 large egg

Grated zest of 1 small lemon

1 teaspoon chopped fresh sage, or ½ teaspoon dried

½ teaspoon fine sea salt

Freshly ground black pepper

¼ cup Homemade Bread Crumbs (page 163), or 2 tablespoons quinoa flakes

¾ pound ground pork

¼ cup white rice flour

2 tablespoons chopped flat-leaf parsley

LENTILS: Warm 1 tablespoon of the olive oil in a saucepan over moderate heat until it shimmers. Add the onion, carrot, and pancetta. Reduce the heat and cook until slightly softened but not colored, about 5 minutes. Add the tomatoes, lentils, and broth. Bring to a boil, cover, reduce the heat to low and simmer until tender, about 45 minutes. Season with salt and pepper to taste.

MEATBALLS: Place the anchovies in a bowl and mash to a paste. Add the egg and beat lightly. Add the lemon zest, sage, salt, a generous grinding of pepper, and the bread crumbs and mix well. Crumble the ground pork into the mixture and combine. Moisten your hands with water, pinch off pieces the size of a walnut, and form into 2-inch balls. Roll the meatballs in the flour.

In a skillet large enough to hold the meatballs in one layer with room to spare, warm the remaining 2 tablespoons of olive oil over moderate heat. Add the meatballs. Brown them quickly and evenly, turning them carefully and shaking the pan occasionally to prevent sticking, about 7 minutes.

Divide the lentils among 4 dinner plates. Top with the meatballs and parsley.

rack of lamb with olive and bread crumb topping

Roasting a rack of lamb briefly at very high heat results in wonderfully juicy, medium-rare meat. The Three-Cheese Cauliflower Gratinato on page 31 makes a great side dish here.

SERVES 4

Preheat the oven to 450°F.

If the lamb racks were encased in Cryovac, rinse them under cold running water and pat dry with paper towels.

Cut all the fat from the top of the racks, right down to the meat. If your butcher hasn't already done so, cut between the ribs, almost down to the meaty nugget, leaving the bones stripped. Cut each rack in half (the meat cooks more evenly this way), to make four servings. Rub each rack with the cut side of the garlic and season the meat lightly with salt and pepper. Place in the roasting pan.

Blend the bread crumbs with the olive oil, parsley, olives, and thyme. Season with pepper. Press the mixture evenly over the meat. Spray lightly with olive oil. Roast for 18 to 20 minutes, until an instant-read meat thermometer (inserted sideways) registers 125°F. (If you prefer medium-cooked lamb, return to the oven for a few more minutes.) Let the lamb rest for 5 minutes before serving on warmed plates.

2 small racks of lamb, 1 pound each, at room temperature

1 fat garlic clove, unpeeled, cut in half

Fine sea salt and freshly ground black pepper

½ cup Homemade Bread Crumbs (page 163)

1 tablespoon extra-virgin olive oil

2 tablespoons chopped flat-leaf parsley

¼ cup pitted and chopped oil-cured black olives

1 teaspoon fresh thyme, or ½ teaspoon dried thyme

Olive oil spray

leg of lamb with anchovy and bread crumb stuffing

This classic, easy-to-carve roast goes especially well with Butternut Squash and Potato Gratinato (page 30) and tender-crisp asparagus spears or slender green beans.

SERVES 6 TO 8

1 boneless leg of lamb, 3½ pounds (see page 149), at room temperature

Fine sea salt and freshly ground black pepper

3 tablespoons olive oil

1 small yellow onion, finely chopped

2 garlic cloves, smashed and chopped

8 canned anchovy fillets, drained

1 tablespoon chopped rosemary

2 tablespoons chopped flat-leaf parsley

¾ cup Homemade Bread Crumbs (page 163)

⅓ cup ricotta

1 cup gluten-free beef broth or chicken broth

Preheat the oven to 400°F.

Spread the meat out on a work surface, fat side down. Season lightly with salt and pepper.

Warm 2 tablespoons of the olive oil in a skillet over moderate heat. Add the onion and sauté until softened but not colored, about 5 minutes. Add the garlic and sauté for 1 minute more. Add the anchovies, mashing them into a paste with a wooden spoon. Stir in the rosemary, parsley, bread crumbs, and a generous grinding of black pepper.

Transfer the stuffing to a bowl and let it cool slightly. Add the ricotta and blend together.

Spread the stuffing over the meat, patting it in place. Roll the meat up and tie tightly with butcher's twine spaced at 1-inch intervals. Make an additional loop lengthways. Place the meat in a roasting pan and rub it with the remaining tablespoon of olive oil.

Roast the lamb, basting two or three times with the pan juices, until an instant-read meat thermometer reaches 130°F, 40 to 45 minutes. Remove the meat to a warm platter and tent it lightly with aluminum foil. Let it rest for 10 to 15 minutes, so the juices can redistribute. The internal temperature will continue to rise another 10 degrees or so for juicy, medium-rare meat.

Meanwhile, discard all but a film of fat from the roasting pan and place the pan over medium-high heat. Add the broth and deglaze, scraping up the brown bits. Reduce the liquid slightly, stirring often, about 5 minutes. Strain into a small saucepan and keep warm.

Carve the meat in fairly thin slices and transfer to heated plates. Add any accumulated juices on the platter to the sauce and taste it for seasoning. Spoon the sauce over the lamb.

TYING A ROLLED ROAST

THESE DAYS, A boned leg of lamb usually comes encased in a stretchy mesh bag that doesn't compact the meat properly for even cooking as it roasts, particularly as it's thick at one end and thin at the other. A better plan is to discard the soggy bag, form an even cylinder, and tie the meat back together firmly with butcher's twine.

It's not always easy to find a very young lamb leg that weighs only 3⅓ pounds after boning. Do this instead: Buy one that weighs 4⅓ pounds. Take the mesh bag off, and lay the meat flat on a work surface, fat side down. Trim off 1 pound of meat from the largest "cushions" to make a much flatter, more even rectangle of meat. This can then be rolled into a narrower cylinder than before and will cook evenly. (If this operation sounds too daunting, explain to the butcher what you want and why, and have him do it. He will be duly impressed, but it's advisable to ask during a slow time in his day.)

Freeze the excess pound of lamb for another purpose, like the Wine-Glazed Meatballs in this chapter. You can grind the cut-up lamb in a food processor (drop in evenly-size cubes of meat with the motor running for an even blend) or chop it very finely.

wine-glazed lamb meatballs with capers

Serve these fine-textured meatballs with polenta or pasta as a main course or pair with an Italian-Style Baguette, page 158, and enjoy a hero sandwich.

SERVES 4

1 pound lean ground lamb

¼ cup Homemade Bread Crumbs (page 163), or 2 tablespoons quinoa flakes

2 tablespoons butter, softened

Fine sea salt and freshly ground black pepper

1 tablespoon chopped fresh marjoram

2 tablespoons capers, drained and rinsed

¼ cup white rice flour

2 tablespoons extra-virgin olive oil

½ cup dry white wine, such as Pinot Grigio

2 tablespoons balsamic vinegar

In a food processor, combine the ground meat, bread crumbs, butter, salt and pepper, and marjoram. Process to a paste. Moisten your fingers with water, pinch off pieces the size of a walnut, and form into balls. Push a couple of capers into the center of each meatball and press together to close. Roll the meatballs in the flour.

In a skillet large enough to hold the meatballs in one layer with room to spare, warm the olive oil over moderate heat. When it shimmers, add the meatballs. Brown quickly and evenly, turning them carefully and shaking the pan occasionally to prevent sticking, about 7 minutes. Using a slotted spoon, transfer the meatballs to a plate.

Pour off all but 2 tablespoons of fat from the pan. Add the wine and vinegar. Lower the heat slightly and reduce the liquid to a glaze of about ½ cup, stirring with a wooden spoon to incorporate the browned bits from the pan, about 5 minutes. Be careful not to overheat or reduce too far, or the glaze may sputter and spit.

Return the meatballs to the pan, roll in the glaze, and heat through, about 1 minute.

lamb stew with fennel, roman style

Italian cooks often use salted anchovies as a seasoning, a culinary echo of ancient Rome when garum, a salty condiment made from fermented and brined fish innards, was used in just about everything. In small quantities, canned anchovies don't add a "fishy" taste at all; it's more of a salty richness. Serve with Italian-Style Baguette (page 158) for mopping up the rich sauce that forms with this stew.

SERVES 4 TO 6

Cut the meat into 1½-inch chunks, discarding excess fat.

Warm the olive oil in a heavy pan over moderate heat. Add the lamb and sauté until well browned, about 7 minutes. Do this in batches if necessary.

Add the fennel and continue cooking until it softens slightly, about 5 minutes. Season lightly with salt and pepper. Add the rosemary and garlic. Sprinkle the flour over the meat, and turn the pieces over so they combine with the pan juices. Add the wine and bring to a boil. Reduce the heat to low, cover the pan, and simmer for 45 minutes.

In a small bowl, combine the anchovies with the wine vinegar and mash to dissolve. Stir into the lamb. Add the orange zest and continue cooking, covered, until the meat is tender, about 30 minutes more.

Check often, and if the sauce is evaporating too much, add a little water, but keep in mind that the sauce should be concentrated and there shouldn't be too much of it.

3 pounds boneless lamb shoulder

1 tablespoon extra-virgin olive oil

2 fennel bulbs, trimmed and chopped into 1-inch chunks

Fine sea salt and freshly ground black pepper

1 tablespoon chopped rosemary

2 garlic cloves, chopped

1 tablespoon white rice flour

1 cup dry white wine, such as Pinot Grigio

3 anchovy fillets, chopped

1 tablespoon wine vinegar

Zest of ½ orange, cut in thin julienne

drunken beef

One of the best beef dishes imaginable, this tender, rich-tasting beef stew goes best with mashed potatoes. A green salad to follow balances the meal perfectly.

SERVES 6

4 tablespoons extra-virgin olive oil

3½ pounds well-marbled beef chuck, trimmed and cut into 2 x 3 x ½-inch thick slices (see below)

Fine sea salt and freshly ground black pepper

2 yellow onions, halved and sliced

2 ounces chopped pancetta or unsmoked bacon (salt pork)

¾ cup full-bodied red wine, such as Chianti Classico or Barolo

2 cups gluten-free beef broth, plus extra if needed

1 teaspoon dried oregano

2 bay leaves

3 garlic cloves, chopped

4 canned anchovies, drained

1 tablespoon capers, rinsed and drained

1 tablespoon cornstarch mixed with 1 tablespoon cold water

Hot mashed potatoes

Preheat the oven to 325°F. Have ready a 3-quart, stovetop-safe, covered casserole, preferably enameled cast iron.

Warm the oil over moderate heat in a large sauté pan. Brown the beef in batches on both sides, about 7 minutes for the first batch (subsequent ones will brown more quickly), seasoning lightly with salt and black pepper. Transfer to the casserole.

Add the onions and pancetta to the pan and sauté until the onions turn light golden, about 5 minutes, and transfer the onion mixture to the casserole. Add the wine to the pan. Let it reduce by one-third, scraping up the tasty brown bits.

Add the broth, oregano, bay leaves, and garlic and bring to a boil. Pour over the beef and onions and mix gently. Cover and bake until the meat is tender, about 2½ hours.

Place the casserole over low heat on top of the stove. If the sauce has cooked down too much, add more beef broth: the liquid should be just below the surface of the meat.

Mash the anchovies in a small bowl and add the capers and cornstarch mixture. Stir the anchovy mixture into the beef and let it bubble until the sauce thickens slightly and clears, 30 seconds or less. Taste for seasoning, and adjust as needed.

 BEEF STEW TACTICS

ASK YOUR BUTCHER to slice well-marbled boneless beef chuck into ½-inch thick slices. When you get it home, divide each slice into pieces approximately 2 x 3 inches, following the natural divisions of the meat. Some bits will be smaller, which is fine. Discard the excess hard white fat and any gristle. Browning flat slices of meat is faster and more efficient as there's more surface available for developing a tasty crust.

oxtail with pine nuts and raisins over creamy polenta

Succulent oxtail is one of the most flavorful parts of a steer. The secret is to cook and refrigerate the meat the day before you plan to serve it. The flavor becomes even richer, and the fat rises and solidifies for easy removal. Served over creamy, golden polenta, it makes memorable comfort food.

SERVES 6

Preheat the oven to 400°F.

Grease a roasting pan with 1 tablespoon of the olive oil and arrange the oxtail pieces in it in a single layer, slightly separated. Roast, turning once, until well browned, about 30 minutes.

Warm the remaining 2 tablespoons of olive oil in a large, heavy pot over moderate heat. Add the onions and sauté until translucent but not colored, 5 minutes. Add the pancetta and sauté until lightly browned, about 2 minutes. Stir in the carrots, celery, and oregano. Sauté for 5 minutes, until slightly softened, and stir in the stock. Bring to a simmer. Using tongs, add the oxtail to the pot.

Place the roasting pan over moderate heat. Deglaze with the wine, scraping up the browned bits with a wooden spoon. Add this liquid to the pot, and season with the salt and a generous grinding of pepper.

Cover and simmer gently until the meat is very tender and pulls from the bones easily, 3½ to 4 hours. Let the mixture cool and pick all the meat off the bones. Refrigerate the meat and sauce separately overnight.

Scrape the layer of fat off the sauce, which sets into a flavorful amber jelly, and discard it. Transfer the sauce to a pot, add the raisins, and bring to a simmer over medium-low heat. Add the oxtail meat and pine nuts and heat through. Stir in the cornstarch mixture and let it bubble until the sauce thickens a little and clears, 20 seconds or less. Taste for seasoning.

Pour a pool of polenta onto each serving plate and top with the oxtail sauce.

3 tablespoons extra-virgin olive oil

4 pounds oxtail, sliced about 2½ inches thick

2 yellow onions, finely chopped

2 ounces diced pancetta or unsmoked bacon (salt pork)

2 carrots, diced

2 celery ribs, de-stringed and finely chopped

1 teaspoon dried oregano

1½ cups gluten-free beef stock

1½ cups full-bodied red wine, such as Chianti Classico or Barolo

1 teaspoon fine sea salt

Freshly ground black pepper

3 tablespoons raisins

3 tablespoons pine nuts

2 tablespoons cornstarch mixed with 2 tablespoons cold water

Creamy Polenta (page 154)

creamy polenta

If you prefer, instead of adding the dry cornmeal to the boiling broth, you can mix it with 1 cup of the water, and stir this slurry into the hot liquid.

SERVES 6

3 cups gluten-free chicken broth

3 cups water

1½ cups polenta

1 tablespoon fine sea salt

3 tablespoons unsalted butter, at room temperature, cut up

½ cup heavy cream, at room temperature

Combine the broth and water in a 2-quart saucepan and bring to a boil.

Add the polenta into the broth in a very thin stream, whisking to prevent lumps, until the mixture returns to a boil. Reduce the heat to low, cover, and cook, stirring occasionally with a wooden spoon, until the mixture is creamy and thick, about 30 minutes. If it should become too solid, blend in a little hot water.

Stir in the salt, butter, and cream and serve at once.

breads, pizza, and crostini

BREAD IS SO fundamental in our culture and so laden with symbolism, that it's unthinkable to be without it. It's the defining food that separates the gluten-intolerant from everyone else, but as newly diagnosed celiacs and the wheat-intolerant swiftly discover, much of the gluten-free bread available in health food stores is both disappointing and expensive.

The good news is that it's remarkably easy to make gluten-free loaves in your own kitchen that look and taste as though they came from a boutique bakery. It's difficult to feel deprived when breaking apart a crusty Italian-Style Baguette (page 158), nibbling on warm, golden Focaccia with Black Olives (page 160), or topping slices of walnut-studded multi-grain bread (page 164) with butter and honey.

quick rustic flatbread

This low, round hearth bread has a crisp crust and a soft, supple crumb that makes it perfect for everything from serving with cheese to sopping up good sauces. To use for sandwiches, cut the loaf in quarters, then slice horizontally.

MAKES 2 FLATBREADS

Preheat the oven to 400°F. Line a baking sheet with parchment paper.

Combine the rice flour, almond meal, tapioca starch, potato starch, salt, baking powder, baking soda, and xanthan gum in a large bowl and stir to blend. In a separate small bowl, beat the egg and whisk in the oil, yogurt, and water.

Using a plastic spatula, stir the liquid ingredients into the flour mixture. Stir hard briefly to form a sticky batter that just holds it shape.

Transfer to the baking sheet, forming two heaps 5 inches apart. Sprinkle lightly with rice flour and pat into 6-inch diameter mounds. Dipping your fingertips in flour, "nudge" the edges of each loaf to make them rounded and smooth. (If they are too thin, they will harden.) Using a single-sided razor blade or sharp knife, slash the loaves from side to side in a cross, ½ inch deep, which encourages rising.

Bake for about 25 minutes, until golden-brown. Transfer the loaves to a wire rack to cool. You can freeze and reheat any leftovers.

VARIATION: For a white loaf, substitute white rice flour for the brown rice flour, and 2 ounces (⅓ cup) of blanched almonds ground in a clean coffee mill for the almond meal. Both these flatbreads make good bread crumbs.

⅓ cup (2 ounces) brown rice flour, plus extra for tops of loaves

½ cup (2 ounces) almond meal

½ cup (2 ounces) tapioca starch

½ cup (3 ounces) potato starch

¾ teaspoon fine sea salt

1 teaspoon baking powder

¼ teaspoon baking soda

1 teaspoon xanthan gum

1 large egg

1 tablespoon canola oil

½ cup plain European-style yogurt (not the condensed Greek variety)

½ cup sparkling or plain water

MEASUREMENTS MATTER

WHEN IT COMES to baking gluten-free breads, flour-to-liquid ratios do matter, so I've included weights as well as the usual cup measurements in all the baking recipes that follow. An inexpensive kitchen scale is one the best investments you will ever make—it's far quicker to weigh ingredients than use cupfuls of this or that, and you get consistent results.

italian-style baguettes

In Tuscany, professional Italian bakers produce long loaves called filone shaped much like a French baguette. This tempting gluten-free version has a thin, golden crust and an airy, supple interior. The unbaked dough is very soft, so you'll need a double baguette pan, available in any kitchenware shop, to support the loaves.

MAKES 2 BAGUETTES

½ cup (3 ounces) white rice flour

½ cup (2½ ounces) tapioca starch

⅓ cup (2 ounces) potato starch

2 tablespoons buckwheat flour or corn starch

2 tablespoons dried milk powder (not instant)

1 teaspoon fine sea salt

1 teaspoon baking powder

¼ teaspoon baking soda

1 teaspoon xanthan gum

1 large egg

1 tablespoon extra-virgin olive oil

½ cup plain European-style yogurt (not the condensed Greek kind)

½ cup sparkling or plain water

plus extra water for smoothing loaves

Preheat the oven to 400°F. Line a double baguette pan with parchment paper, creasing the center and edges to make it lie snug.

Combine the rice flour, tapioca starch, potato starch, buckwheat flour, milk powder, salt, baking powder, baking soda, and xanthan gum in a large bowl and stir to blend. In a separate bowl, beat the egg and whisk in the olive oil, yogurt, and water. Using a plastic spatula, stir the liquid ingredients into the flour mixture. Stir hard briefly to make a smooth batter that just holds its shape.

Drop small, tear-shaped dollops of batter in the double pan, overlapping them slightly to form two humpy rows about 12 inches long. (This takes a little practice, but even if you make irregular blobs, you'll still get delicious bread.) Moisten the spatula lightly with water and smooth the surface, following the shapes of the humps, but don't squish out the air.

Bake for about 25 minutes, until golden and crusty. Slide the loaves out of the lined pan onto the oven rack and bake for another 10 minutes to let them dry out and turn a deeper gold. Transfer the loaves to a wire rack and let cool. Heat briefly before serving to re-crisp the crust.

TIP: As with French baguettes, this bread doesn't keep, but it freezes well either whole or sliced. If intended for crostini, leave the freshly baked loaves out for several hours before slicing on the diagonal.

GLUTEN-FREE FLOUR MIXTURES

It might seem odd to have to use several different gluten-free flours to make a loaf of bread, but just one kind of "alternative" flour won't do the job. Each variety makes a specific contribution.

However, because gluten-free breads, cakes, cookies, and pie dough all require different flour mixtures to be at their best, and as cakes and most cookies don't need xanthan gum, I don't recommend making an "all-purpose" gluten-free baking blend. Instead, I list all the ingredients used in each recipe.

This way, should you happen to have additional food allergies, or just don't have a particular flour on hand, it's easy to substitute other flours with a similar texture, say potato starch for cornstarch, coconut flour for almond flour, or millet flour for corn flour.

To save time, when you've tried a bread recipe that you know you'll want to make often, assemble the dry ingredients separately for several loaves, label the bags (very important!), and toss them in the freezer for up to 6 months. Every bag gets the right amount of each flour, xanthan gum, and leavening, and they're ready to use.

focaccia with black olives

Crispy and chewy at the same time, this golden-brown flatbread makes an outstanding snack with a glass of wine. A very ancient bread, focaccia gets its name from the Latin word for hearth, focus, as flatbreads were originally baked on a hot hearthstone.

Serves 8

³/₄ cup (3 ounces) whole-grain, stone-ground corn flour, such as Bob's Red Mill

¹/₂ cup (3 ounces) white rice flour

¹/₂ cup (2¹/₂ ounces) tapioca starch

1 tablespoon dried milk powder (not instant)

1 teaspoon baking powder

¹/₄ teaspoon baking soda

1 teaspoon xanthan gum

¹/₂ teaspoon fine sea salt

1 large egg, plus 1 beaten egg white for glaze

1 cup sparkling or plain water

1 teaspoon apple cider vinegar

1 tablespoon extra-virgin olive oil

2 teaspoons chopped rosemary

12 oil-cured black olives, pitted and roughly chopped

¹/₄ to ¹/₂ teaspoon coarse sea salt crystals

Preheat the oven to 400°F. Line a baking sheet with parchment paper.

Combine the corn flour, rice flour, tapioca starch, dried milk, baking powder, baking soda, xanthan gum, and salt and stir well. In a separate bowl, beat the egg and stir in the water, vinegar, olive oil, rosemary, and olives.

Pour the liquid ingredients over the flour mixture and stir hard with a plastic spatula for a few seconds until a soft dough forms that barely holds its shape.

Place in two mounds on the baking sheet and lightly smooth into ovals approximately 8¹/₂ x 4¹/₂ inches. Brush with the egg-white glaze, gently smoothing the surface and edges. Sprinkle with the salt crystals.

Bake for about 25 minutes, until golden-brown. Transfer to a wire rack, and enjoy while still warm.

instant polenta skillet bread

The secret here is baking this aromatic corn bread in a preheated heavy iron pan.
Serve the bread warm to accompany a meal or with assorted olives as an appetizer.

MAKES 8 WEDGES

Preheat the oven to 450°F and heat a well-seasoned 8½-inch blue steel crêpe pan or iron skillet at the same time.

Combine the polenta, corn flour, cornstarch, xanthan gum, baking soda, baking powder, and salt. In a separate bowl, whisk together the buttermilk, eggs, ½ cup of the Parmesan, and 1½ tablespoons of the corn oil.

Protecting your hand with a mitt, remove the hot pan from the oven. Add the remaining ½ tablespoon corn oil and swirl it around to coat the bottom of the pan.

Pour the liquid ingredients over the dry ingredients, mix until smooth, and scrape the batter into the hot, oiled pan. Top with the remaining tablespoon of the Parmesan and a generous grinding of black pepper.

Transfer the pan to the oven and bake for about 12 minutes, until golden-brown. Loosen the sides of the bread with a knife tip and turn it out onto a wire rack. Let it cool for 10 minutes before cutting it into wedges.

¼ cup instant polenta (2 ounces) such as Beretta, or fine stone-ground cornmeal, such as Arrowhead Mills

½ cup (2 ounces) stone-ground corn flour, such as Bob's Red Mill

¼ cup (1½ ounces) cornstarch

½ teaspoon xanthan gum

¼ teaspoon baking soda

½ teaspoon baking powder

½ teaspoon fine sea salt

½ cup buttermilk (or ¼ cup each plain European-style yogurt and milk)

2 large eggs

2 ounces (about ½ cup) coarsely grated Parmigiano-Reggiano, plus 1 tablespoon

2 tablespoons corn oil

Freshly ground black pepper

milk bread

While you won't find anything like this in an Italian bakery, this light and mellow gluten-free loaf is useful for making the homemade bread crumbs so essential in many Italian recipes, as well as crostini and croutons. It's yeast-raised, so have all the ingredients at room temperature to aid rising. (If need be, mix the flours and warm in a low oven and warm the unshelled eggs in hot water.) The recipe is easy to double, but be sure to use two regular loaf pans rather than a single large one.

MAKES 1 LOAF

⅓ cup (2 ounces) white rice flour

⅓ cup (2 ounces) potato starch

⅓ cup (2 ounces) tapioca starch

½ cup (2 ounces) stone-ground corn flour, such as Bob's Red Mill

3 tablespoons (1 ounce) dried milk powder (not instant)

1 teaspoon active dry yeast

1 teaspoon xanthan gum

½ teaspoon fine sea salt

1 large egg

1 large egg white

½ cup whole or part-skim milk mixed with ½ cup water, heated to 110°F.

1 tablespoon unsalted butter, softened

Line an 8 x 4-inch loaf pan with a 7 x 10-inch sheet of parchment paper. It's fine to leave the short sides uncovered.

Combine the white rice flour, potato starch, tapioca starch, corn flour, milk powder, yeast, xanthan gum, and salt in the bowl of an electric stand mixer.

In a separate bowl, whisk the egg and egg white together.

Start mixing the flours with the K-shaped flat beater and slowly add the egg mixture. Continue blending at low speed until well mixed, about 1 minute. Add the milk mixture, then the butter, and mix at medium-high speed until the dough starts to hold its shape and forms "strings," about 5 minutes.

Using a plastic spatula, transfer the very soft dough to the lined pan (it will be about one-third full). Cover with the pan with plastic wrap and let the dough rise in a warm place until doubled in bulk, about 1¼ hours.

Preheat the oven to 375°F. Bake the loaf for about 40 minutes, until well risen and golden-brown. Remove from the oven, loosen the short sides of the loaf, and lift it out of the pan using the parchment paper as a sling.

Return the loaf to the oven, paper and all, and turn off the heat. Let the loaf dry for a further 10 minutes. Transfer the bread to a wire rack and let it cool for at least 2 hours before cutting.

HOMEMADE BREAD CRUMBS
AND CROUTONS

TO MAKE THE best gluten-free bread crumbs, use the interior of day-old Milk Bread (page 162) or Quick Rustic Flatbread (page 157).

Shave the crust off the loaf and discard. Dice the soft interior, transfer to a food processor, and process to form coarse crumbs. Should they feel slightly moist, spread them out on a cookie sheet and let them dry at room temperature for a few hours. Place in a glass screw-top jar or resealable plastic bag and store in the freezer. The crumbs won't freeze into a solid block and are ready to use.

Be cautious about making bread crumbs or croutons from the gluten-free bread found in refrigerator/freezer cases at natural foods stores. Most are heavily sweetened (in addition to other shortcomings) and not suitable for incorporating into savory dishes. Notable exceptions, so far, are Glutino's Gluten Free Fiber Bread and Gluten Free Flax Bread. Both these very acceptable loaves have a light texture and a mellow flavor that doesn't interfere with other ingredients, and they make good toast.

Packaged gluten-free bread crumbs are available, at considerable expense, but again, be cautious. Some brands, although labeled as bread crumbs, turn out to be very fine cracker crumbs. Unlike crumbled bread, they are not absorbent and are hopeless for anything except coating fish or chicken before frying, in which case you might just as well use rice flour.

To prepare croutons for salads, cut the soft interior of day-old Milk Bread or Quick Rustic Flatbread into 3/4-inch cubes. Let the cubes dry for a few hours at room temperature, then bag and freeze. Fry, unthawed is fine, just before using.

quick multigrain bread with walnuts

Rustic multigrain loaves are enjoying new popularity with health-conscious bread lovers in Italy as well as in the United States. This gluten-free version pairs well with cheese and fruit or a hearty minestrone.

MAKES 1 FLATBREAD

½ cup (2½ ounces) walnut pieces, coarsely chopped

½ cup (2 ounces) stone-ground, whole-grain corn flour, such as Bob's Red Mill

¼ cup (1 ounce) flax meal

½ cup (3 ounces) brown rice flour

½ cup (2½ ounces) tapioca starch

1 teaspoon xanthan gum

1 teaspoon baking powder

¼ teaspoon baking soda

1 teaspoon fine sea salt

2 large eggs

1 tablespoon extra-virgin olive oil

½ cup plain yogurt (not condensed Greek variety)

½ cup sparkling or plain water

Olive oil spray

Preheat the oven to 400°F. Line a baking sheet with parchment paper.

Combine the walnuts, corn flour, flax meal, brown rice flour, tapioca starch, xanthan gum, baking powder, baking soda, and salt and stir well. In a separate bowl, beat together the eggs, olive oil, yogurt, and water.

Pour the liquid ingredients over the flour mixture and stir hard with a plastic spatula for a few seconds until a soft dough forms that barely holds its shape. Place in a mound on the baking sheet and smooth into a slightly domed, 8-inch diameter circle.

Spray lightly with olive oil and gently smooth the surface and edges. Using a single-sided razor blade or a sharp knife, slash a diagonal grid pattern at 2-inch intervals over the surface.

Bake for about 30 minutes, until brown and crusty. Let cool on a wire rack before slicing.

TIP: Slice this nut-studded bread across, and freeze. The long, biscotti-shaped slices can be toasted while still frozen in a pre-heated ridged grill pan or heavy skillet in a just couple of minutes. Wonderful at breakfast time with butter or fresh goat cheese and honey, this bread is also ideal for crostini.

breadsticks

Unlike commercially made breadsticks, which are crunchy all the way through, these treats are literally golden sticks of bread, crisp on the outside and soft within. The contrast of textures and the toasty flavor makes them irresistible. To serve, place them upright in a jug, like a bouquet.

MAKES 12 BREADSTICKS

Preheat the oven to 425°F. Line a large baking sheet with parchment paper.

Combine the rice flour, tapioca starch, salt, baking powder, and xanthan gum in a large bowl. In a separate small bowl, blend the egg, milk, water, olive oil, and vinegar and whisk until smooth.

Pour the liquid ingredients over the flour mixture. Using a plastic spatula, stir briskly for about 30 seconds, until the dough is smooth and just holds it shape. (Energetic stirring activates the xanthan gum, which thickens the runny batter.)

Transfer the dough to a pastry bag fitted with a plain round ½-inch metal tip, or use a resealable plastic bag with one corner snipped off. Working across the short side of the baking sheet and pressing lightly, form twelve 9-inch-long sticks, 1 inch apart. Lightly brush the tops of the breadsticks with the beaten egg white, and sprinkle with the poppy seeds.

Bake for about 25 minutes, until golden and fragrant. Transfer to a wire rack. Serve warm or reheat. These breadsticks will keep frozen for up to two months.

³/₄ cup (4½ ounces) white rice flour

³/₄ cup (3¾ ounces) tapioca starch

1 teaspoon fine sea salt

1 teaspoon baking powder

1 teaspoon xanthan gum

1 large egg, plus 1 beaten egg white for glaze

½ cup whole or part-skim milk

½ cup sparkling or plain water

1 tablespoon extra-virgin olive oil

1 teaspoon cider vinegar

Poppy seeds, coarse sea salt crystals, or sesame seeds, for sprinkling

quick rice flour pizza dough

Essentially a flatbread with a savory topping, pizza has an ancient history. One story has it that the ancient Greek colonizers of Neapolis (present-day Naples) made pita bread in their new home, and the word evolved into pizza.

Unlike American take-out pizza, which is all about the gooey filling and takes the place of dinner, this pizza is all about the bread and makes a peerless appetizer with a glass of wine. This crust has a crisp base and a rounded, chewy-crispy rim. Before you reach for the marinara sauce, do try these pizzette with nothing more than some flavorful cheese and black olives. (Too much moisture will make any crust soggy.)

MAKES TWO 7-INCH ROUND PIZZA BASES,
SERVES 6 TO 8 AS AN APPETIZER

⅓ cup (2 ounces) brown rice flour

⅓ cup (2 ounces) white rice flour

½ cup (2½ ounces) tapioca starch

1 tablespoon dried milk powder (not instant)

1 teaspoon fine sea salt

1 teaspoon baking powder

1 teaspoon xanthan gum

1 cup sparkling or plain water

1 tablespoon extra-virgin olive oil

1 teaspoon cider vinegar

1 egg white, lightly beaten

Preheat the oven to 425°F. Line a large baking sheet with parchment paper. Using a plate as a guide, draw two 7-inch diameter circles on the paper with a pencil, slightly separated from each other.

Combine the brown rice flour, white rice flour, tapioca starch, dried milk powder, salt, baking powder, and xanthan gum in a large bowl. In another bowl, blend the water, olive oil, and vinegar and whisk to mix.

Pour the liquid ingredients over the flour mixture. Using a plastic spatula, stir hard briefly to make a smooth, soft batter that just holds its shape.

Transfer slightly less than half the dough to a pastry bag fitted with a plain round ⅓-inch metal tip, or use a resealable plastic bag with one corner snipped off. Divide the remaining dough between the circles marked out on the parchment paper, spreading it thinly with a plastic spatula. Pipe a raised, rounded "rim" around the edge of each one. Brush all over with the egg white, which helps sealing and browning.

Bake until puffed and starting to brown, about 20 minutes. Cover with your pizza topping of choice (try those on the next page or assemble your own favorite combinations) and return to the oven to bake until bubbling hot, about 7 minutes.

cheese and olive pizzette

Divide the Fontina between two prebaked pizza bases and top with the olives, cut side down. Sprinkle with the Parmesan. Return to the oven until the cheese melts and starts to turn golden, about 5 minutes.

½ ounce (about ¼ cup) shredded or thinly sliced Fontina or Gruyère

12 Kalamata or oil-cured black olives, halved and pitted

½ to 1 tablespoon grated Parmigiano-Reggiano

cherry tomato and pancetta pizzette

Scatter the Fontina over the prebaked pizza bases and top with the pancetta and tomatoes, cut side down. Sprinkle with the Parmesan. Return to the oven, and bake until the cheese melts and the pancetta becomes crisp, about 8 minutes. Sprinkle with the bits of basil.

1 ounce (about ¼ cup) shredded or thinly sliced Fontina or Gruyère

6 thin slices pancetta or unsmoked bacon (salt pork), quartered

8 cherry tomatoes, halved

1 tablespoon grated Parmigiano-Reggiano

Roughly torn basil leaves

spiced anchovy bruschetta

The addictive spiced butter used for this bruschetta is wonderful for topping grilled gluten-free bread; a dollop placed on top of a juicy steak or in vegetable soup doesn't go amiss, either. This recipe makes about half a cup and keeps well in the refrigerator. Let it soften a bit before using.

SERVES 6

1 (2-ounce) can anchovy
fillets, drained
and chopped

1 teaspoon brandy

1/8 teaspoon cayenne
or chile powder,
or more to taste

1/8 teaspoon nutmeg,
or more to taste

1/8 teaspoon cinnamon,
or more to taste

5 tablespoons unsalted
butter, cut into cubes,
softened

12 slices day-old
Italian-Style Baguette
(page 158), cut
diagonally
½-inch thick

Olive oil spray

Mash the anchovies in a small bowl. Add the brandy, cayenne, nutmeg, cinnamon, and butter and beat with a wooden spoon until smooth.

Preheat a ridged grill pan or heavy skillet. Spray both sides of the bread slices with olive oil and grill or fry until browned, turning once. Top the grilled bread with the anchovy butter and serve warm or cold.

BRUSCHETTA AND CROSTINI

THESE ARE PRETTY much the same thing: rustic appetizers of chewy, toasted bread anointed with olive oil and spread with a savory topping. In general, bruschetta (from *bruscare*, to toast), are simple; crostini (little crusts) are a little more elaborate. Two bruschetta or crostini appetizers generally make one serving, depending on appetites and size of the bread slices. Plain crostini are also served with soup.

Assuming that a hot outdoor grill is not available, a ridged grill pan or heavy skillet used on top of the stove works well.

For a large number of assorted crostini—which make first-rate but inexpensive party fare—preheat the oven to 375°F. Arrange the slices of bread on a foil-lined baking sheet and spray with olive oil. Turn them over, and spray the second side. Bake until the undersides are lightly browned (the tops will be crisp, but lighter in color), about 8 minutes total. Top with your chosen spreads.

fresh tomato bruschetta

When sweet, vine-ripened tomatoes and fragrant basil become available in summer, take full advantage! To peel tomatoes, cut a cross in the flat end and drop in boiling water for 10 seconds or so. The skins will slip right off.

SERVES 6

Combine the tomatoes, basil, capers, olive oil, and vinegar. Season to taste with salt and pepper.

Preheat a ridged grill pan or heavy skillet. Spray both sides of the bread slices with olive oil and grill or fry until browned, turning once. Rub the grilled bread with garlic and top with the tomato mixture. Garnish with basil leaves.

1 cup peeled, seeded, and chopped vine-ripened tomatoes

2 tablespoons chopped basil, plus tiny leaves for garnish

1 tablespoon capers, rinsed and drained

1 teaspoon extra-virgin olive oil

1 teaspoon red wine vinegar

Fine sea salt and freshly ground black pepper

12 slices day-old Italian-Style Baguette (page 158), cut diagonally ½-inch thick

Olive oil spray

1 large garlic clove, unpeeled, cut in half

olive paste bruschetta

A Mediterranean favorite, olive paste—also known as tapenade—can be used as a spread for bruschetta, a sauce for pasta (add more olive oil), or combined with gluten-free bread crumbs and parsley to make a sensational stuffing for roast chicken legs (page 110). This recipe makes about 1½ cups; more than you'll need for twelve bruschetta, but it will keep for ten days or more refrigerated.

Serves 6

2 cups (8 ounces) pitted Kalamata olives, rinsed and drained

12 oil-cured black olives, pitted

1 tablespoon capers, rinsed and drained

2 canned, drained anchovy fillets, mashed

1 small garlic clove, smashed and chopped

2 tablespoons extra-virgin olive oil

12 slices day-old Italian-Style Baguette (page 158), cut diagonally ½-inch thick

Olive oil spray

Combine the Kalamata olives, black olives, capers, anchovies, garlic, and olive oil in a food processor or blender. Process in short, sharp bursts to a chunky purée, scraping down the sides of the bowl as needed.

Preheat a ridged grill pan or heavy skillet. Spray both sides of the bread slices with olive oil and grill or fry until browned, turning once. Top the grilled bread with the olive paste and serve warm or cold.

caramelized grape tomato crostini

For a stunning, unexpected use of tiny grape tomatoes, it's hard to beat roasting them with orange zest. They reduce slightly and take on lots of flavor. Delicious on grilled bread, these tomatoes can also be served as a side dish with chicken or fish. (Larger cherry tomatoes don't work as well here; the skins are too tough.)

SERVES 4

Preheat the oven to 400°F. Combine the tomatoes, orange zest, sugar, and anise seeds in a shallow baking dish just large enough to hold them in one layer (a little crowding is fine). Season with salt and pepper, add the olive oil, and mix well. Roast until the tomatoes start to caramelize, about 20 minutes.

Preheat a ridged grill pan or heavy skillet. Spray both sides of the bread slices with olive oil and grill or fry until browned, turning once. Rub the grilled bread with the garlic, and top with caramelized tomatoes. Serve warm or cold.

½ pound tiny red and/or yellow grape tomatoes, rinsed

Zest of ½ orange, cut in thin julienne

1 teaspoon sugar

Pinch anise seeds

Fine sea salt and freshly ground black pepper

2 tablespoons extra-virgin olive oil

12 to 16 slices day-old Italian-Style Baguette (page 158), sliced diagonally ½-inch thick

Olive oil spray

1 large garlic clove, unpeeled, cut in half

mushroom crostini

As with many crostini toppings, this one is equally good served over rounds of fried or baked polenta as a first course. This recipe makes approximately 1 cup of spread.

SERVES 6

2 tablespoons extra-virgin olive oil

4 canned anchovy fillets, drained

½ pound cremini (brown) mushrooms, finely chopped

½ teaspoon dried thyme

1 garlic clove, chopped

3 tablespoons heavy cream

2 tablespoons chopped flat-leaf parsley

Freshly ground black pepper

Fine sea salt

12 to 16 slices day-old Italian-Style Baguette (page 158), cut diagonally ½-inch thick

Olive oil spray

Heat the oil, add the anchovies, and mash with a wooden spoon. Add the chopped mushrooms, thyme, and garlic and cook until glassy looking and tender, stirring often, about 8 minutes. The mushrooms will reduce considerably. Add the cream, parsley, and a generous grinding of pepper, cook for 1 minute more, and remove from the heat. Taste for seasoning, and add salt as needed.

Preheat a ridged grill pan or heavy skillet. Spray both sides of the bread slices with olive oil and grill or fry until browned, turning once. Top the grilled bread with the mushroom mixture and serve warm.

poor man's caviar crostini

Any resemblance to the best Beluga is fleeting, but this faux caviar is appetizing, eminently affordable, and easy to make. This recipe makes about 1 cup.

Serves 6

Trim the ends of the zucchini and cut in quarters lengthways. Simmer in lightly salted water until barely tender, 3 minutes. Drain and cut into dice. Place in a food processor with the olives, anchovies, capers, olive oil, and a generous grinding of black pepper. Process briefly to make an evenly granular soft spread.

Preheat a ridged grill pan or heavy skillet. Spray both sides of the bread slices with olive oil and grill or fry until browned, turning once. Top the grilled bread with the zucchini mixture. Serve warm or at room temperature.

1 medium zucchini, about 5 ounces

Fine sea salt

3/4 cup pitted Gaeta or Kalamata olives, drained

6 canned anchovy fillets, drained and chopped

1 teaspoon capers, drained

1 tablespoon extra-virgin olive oil

Freshly ground black pepper

12 to 16 slices day-old Italian-Style Baguette (page 158), cut diagonally 1/2-inch thick

Olive oil spray

chicken liver crostini

It's advisable to use chicken livers from humanely reared organic or free-range birds to make this luxurious-tasting spread. For velvety results, be careful not to overcook.

SERVES 6

1 tablespoon olive oil

3 tablespoons unsalted butter

1 small onion, minced

3 canned anchovy fillets, drained

½ pound chicken livers, trimmed and cut in 1-inch chunks

3 fresh sage leaves, or ¼ teaspoon crumbled dried sage

2 tablespoons dry Marsala

Fine sea salt and freshly ground black pepper

12 to 16 slices day-old Italian baguette (page 158), cut diagonally ½-inch thick

Olive oil spray

Warm the olive oil and 2 tablespoons of the butter in a heavy skillet over moderate heat. Add the onion and simmer until starting to turn golden, about 5 minutes. Add the anchovies and mash with a wooden spoon. Add the chicken livers and sage, and sauté until the livers are barely cooked, about 3 minutes. Do not overcook. Add the Marsala and let it almost evaporate.

Using a slotted spoon, transfer the chicken liver mixture to a cutting board. Season lightly with salt and pepper. Using a chef's knife, chop the chicken liver mixture finely. (A food processor would make it too smooth; it should retain some texture.) Heat the remaining tablespoon of butter in the skillet, add the chicken liver mixture, and stir until blended with the sauce remaining in the skillet and heated through, about 20 seconds.

Preheat a ridged grill pan or heavy skillet. Spray both sides of the bread slices with olive oil and grill or fry until browned, turning once. Top the grilled bread with the chicken liver mixture and serve warm or at room temperature.

gorgonzola and walnut crostini

Voluptuously creamy Gorgonzola and toasted walnuts make a fabulous combination for topping crostini. For the bread, use either Italian-Style Baguette (page 158) or slices of Quick Multigrain Bread with Walnuts (page 164) cut in halves or thirds.

SERVES 6

Preheat the oven to 350°F.

Spread the walnuts on a rimmed baking sheet and bake until lightly toasted and fragrant, about 8 minutes. Chop coarsely.

Preheat a ridged grill pan or heavy skillet. Spray both sides of the bread slices with olive oil and grill or fry until browned, turning once. Immediately cover the grilled bread with the sliced Gorgonzola, so it can melt in slightly. Top with the chopped walnuts, pressing them in lightly and serve the crostini while still warm.

½ cup (2½ ounces) walnut halves and pieces

12 to 16 slices of Italian-Style Baguette (page 158), cut diagonally ½-inch thick

Olive oil spray

3 to 4 ounces Italian Gorgonzola, thinly sliced

anchovy and white cheese crostini

Bold flavors and contrasting crispy-creamy textures make these simple crostini a big favorite. This recipe makes about 1¼ cups of topping; refrigerate the extra—it will keep for a couple of days—and serve as a dip with bite-sized raw veggies.

SERVES 6

1 cup cottage cheese
(not nonfat)

2 ounces fresh white
goat cheese, crumbled

1 small garlic clove,
smashed and
finely chopped

1-2 tablespoons chopped
flat-leaf parsley

2-3 teaspoons capers,
rinsed and drained,
chopped if large

Freshly ground
black pepper

6-8 canned anchovy
fillets, drained and cut in
half crossways

12-16 slices of day-old
Italian-Style Baguette
(page 158), cut
diagonally, 1/2-inch thick

Olive oil spray

Place the cottage cheese, goat cheese, and garlic in a food processor and process until very smooth, scraping down the bowl as needed. Add the parsley, capers, and a generous grinding of black pepper. Pulse to mix, and transfer to a small bowl.

Preheat a ridged grill pan or heavy skillet. Spray both sides of the bread slices with olive oil and grill or fry until browned, turning once. Spread the grilled bread with the cheese mixture and top with half an anchovy. Serve warm or at room temperature.

sweet things

A HUGE REPERTOIRE OF wonderful bakery and dessert items exists in Italy, and happily for us, many of the most delicious ones can be tweaked to make them gluten-free.

Some Italian desserts are regional, such as the buttery Rum-Raisin Genoa Cake on page 180, or seasonal, like the voluptuous Fresh Fig or Strawberry Tart on page 208. Others appear only during special festivals, and sometimes date back centuries. Panforte (page 210)—Siena's signature sweetmeat made with dried fruits, spices, nuts, and honey—is at least eight centuries old and still a treat today.

Of all the tempting cookies you will find in this chapter, don't miss the deceptively simple Golden Raisin and Cornmeal Cookies on page 200. Based on a classic from northern Italy, they're like peanuts: it's impossible to eat just one. The crispy-chewy *brutti ma buoni* ("ugly but good") Chocolate Meringue Cookies with the soft chocolate interiors on page 202 also beg for attention, as do the feather-light Almond Macaroons (Amaretti) on page 190.

almond-ricotta cake

A rustic cake with a moist, dense texture that hints of marzipan, this torta is rich with almond meal, whole-grain cornmeal, eggs, and ricotta. Who knew that dessert could be so nutritious?

SERVES 10

Preheat the oven to 350°F. Grease the sides of a 9-inch cake pan with butter and line the base with a circle of parchment paper. Butter that, too.

Using a clean electric coffee mill and working in batches, grind the cornmeal to make it finer. Alternatively, use a food processor and process for 5 minutes. Combine the cornmeal with the almond meal, confectioners' sugar, baking powder, and salt, and mix well.

Beat the butter and sugar until light and fluffy, then beat in the ricotta. Beat in the eggs, almond extract, and lemon zest. Put the cornmeal mixture into a coarse sieve, sift half of it over the butter mixture, and fold in with a plastic spatula. Repeat with the remainder.

Transfer to the cake pan, smooth the top, and bake for about 30 minutes, until the cake is golden and an inserted toothpick emerges clean.

Let the cake cool in the pan for 5 minutes, then loosen the sides with a knife blade and unmold. Peel off the parchment paper, and let the cake cool completely, right side up, on a wire cake rack. Dust with confectioners' sugar before serving.

Butter for cake pan

¾ cup (3½ ounces) fine stone-ground cornmeal, such as Arrowhead Mills

1 cup (4 ounces) almond meal

½ cup (2½ ounces) confectioners' sugar, plus more for top of cake

1 teaspoon baking powder

Pinch fine sea salt

8 tablespoons (4 ounces) unsalted butter, softened

½ cup (4 ounces) sugar

6 ounces ricotta

4 large eggs

1 teaspoon almond extract

Grated zest of 1 small lemon

Confectioners' sugar

rum-raisin genoa cake

Essentially a moist, buttery coffee cake, Genoa cake is traditionally made with ground almonds and cornstarch or potato starch, not wheat flour. It's especially good when made with rum-soaked raisins. For the best texture, be sure the butter, eggs, and almond meal are at room temperature.

SERVES 8

⅓ cup (2 ounces) raisins

2 tablespoons dark rum

9 tablespoons (4½ ounces) unsalted butter, plus extra for pan, softened

¾ cup (6 ounces) sugar

3 large eggs

½ teaspoon vanilla extract

Pinch fine sea salt

1 cup (4 ounces) almond meal

2 tablespoons (1 ounce) potato starch

Confectioners' sugar

Preheat the oven to 350°F. Grease the sides of an 8-inch square cake pan with butter, line the bottom with parchment paper, and butter that, too.

Combine the raisins and rum in a small saucepan and heat gently, stirring, until the liquid almost evaporates, about 2 minutes. Remove from the heat and let the raisins cool to lukewarm.

Beat the butter and sugar together until creamy. Add the eggs one at a time, beating after each addition. Add the vanilla and salt. Blend in the almond meal with the potato starch and beat in. Fold in the rum-soaked raisins.

Spread the batter in the prepared pan. Bake for about 30 minutes, until risen and golden-brown and an inserted toothpick emerges clean. Place the pan on a wire rack and let the cake cool for 10 minutes. Unmold, peel off the parchment paper and let the cake cool completely, right side up. When ready to serve, cut into 16 bars, but do not separate. Dust with confectioners' sugar and then transfer the bars to a plate. Serves 2 bars per person.

NUT FLOURS—BE YOUR OWN MILLER

WHILE IT'S POSSIBLE to buy nut flours/nut meals, it's usually cheaper to make your own, and they'll have more flavor because they're fresh.

For the best results, use a hand-cranked nut mill. Available in kitchenware stores such as Williams-Sonoma, look for the rotary action one made by Zyliss that looks like a miniature meat grinder. It creates fluffy nut flour (or ground chocolate) that promotes higher-rising cakes.

Another option is to use an electric coffee mill dedicated to items other than coffee. True, these mills don't hold much, but they create nut flour very quickly.

Unfortunately, food processors work on a different principle and make oily little granules instead of fluffy flakes. This is great for cookies, but not so good for most cakes. If a food processor is your only option, process the nuts with some of the flour, starch, or sugar listed in the recipe to take up the released nut oil and be careful not to grind the mixture into a nut paste.

Always store highly perishable nut flours in the freezer (they will keep frozen for up to six months), but bring this and all cake ingredients to room temperature before baking, for better rising. Cookie and pie doughs, on the other hand, are best kept cold.

Keep in mind that 1 cup of whole almonds weighs 6 ounces, but 1 cup of fluffy nut flour weighs only 4 ounces. See page 216 for more commonly used baking ingredient measurements. A kitchen scale is really worth buying; using cup measures is inherently inexact. Professional bakers always go by weights for consistent results. It's also quicker than scooping and leveling ingredients.

almond-pumpkin cake

Naturally sweet canned pumpkin lends an indefinable fruitiness to this feather-light cake, but no one can identify what the magic ingredient might be. It makes a brilliant choice for a suitably festive but not overly rich Thanksgiving dessert.

SERVES 8

Butter for cake pan

1 cup (4 ounces) almond meal

3 tablespoons (1½ ounces) potato starch

½ teaspoon cinnamon

4 large eggs

1 cup (8 ounces) sugar

¼ cup (2 ounces) canned unsweetened pumpkin purée

Confectioners' sugar

WHIPPED ALMOND CREAM (OPTIONAL)

½ cup heavy cream

2 tablespoons confectioners' sugar

½ teaspoon almond extract

Preheat the oven to 350°F. Butter the sides of a 9-inch round cake pan, line the bottom with parchment paper, and butter that, too.

Combine the almond meal, potato starch, and cinnamon in a large bowl.

In a separate bowl, beat the eggs lightly to combine; then beat in the sugar little by little. Beat at medium-high speed until the mixture reaches the ribbon stage, about 7 minutes. (See "Bakers' Secrets," page 183.)

Using a plastic spatula, lightly fold in the pumpkin purée; leaving streaks is fine. Sprinkle half the almond meal mixture around the edges of the bowl to avoid deflating the batter and fold in. Repeat with the remaining almond meal mixture.

Transfer the batter to the cake pan. Bake for about 30 minutes, until the cake is golden and shrinks away slightly from the sides of the pan and an inserted toothpick emerges clean. Let the cake cool in the pan for 5 minutes. Run a knife blade round the edge of the cake to loosen it, then turn out onto a wire cake rack. Peel off the parchment paper and let the cake cool right side up.

To make the Whipped Almond Cream, if using, whip the cream to the soft peak stage. Add the confectioners' sugar and almond extract and beat just until the cream is stiff enough to hold its shape softly. Dust the cake with confectioners' sugar before serving, and pass the Whipped Almond Cream separately.

TIP: You will have an almost full can of pumpkin purée left over. Include this in Off-the-Shelf White Bean, Sage, and Pumpkin Soup (page 50) the next day.

BAKERS' SECRETS:
USING AIR TO MAKE CAKES LIGHT

Beat to the Ribbon Stage

Pastry chefs introduce air into cake batters by beating the eggs and sugar together until the emulsion is so thick that a lifted beater will leave a slowly dissolving trail, or ribbon. This thick liaison holds up other ingredients, like flour or nut meal, and helps to promote a light and even texture. (And all that oxygen trapped inside the cake helps to bring out the flavors when it's devoured.)

Fold In

In bakers' jargon, this is just shorthand for incorporating one ingredient into another without deflating the batter. If you simply stirred flour into an egg-sugar liaison, you would drive out the air and your baked cake would be dense and heavy. To avoid this calamity, either sift your flour over the surface or sprinkle heavier ingredients like ground nuts or purées around the edge of the bowl. Next, using a plastic spatula, slice downwards through the batter and then turn your wrist and scoop upwards from the bottom of the bowl. Repeat this motion while simultaneously rotating the bowl with your other hand. This way, you can quickly incorporate ingredients while losing a minimum of air.

walnut cake with lemon cream

Every region in Italy seems to have its own version of a walnut flour cake or torta di noci. This one is served with an addictive, sweet-sharp lemon sauce. Fresh blueberries or raspberries go well with this luxurious dessert. Make the lemon curd ahead of time, as it has to cool.

SERVES 8 TO 10

Butter for cake pan

2/3 cup (3 ounces) walnut halves and pieces

1 cup (8 ounces) sugar

1/3 cup (2 ounces) potato starch

2/3 cup (4 ounces) almonds

Pinch fine sea salt

1/2 teaspoon baking powder

4 large eggs

Grated zest of 1 small lemon

Confectioners' sugar

LEMON CREAM

4 ounces mascarpone

1 cup Lemon Curd (page 185, or use a purchased brand made with butter)

Heat the oven to 350°F. Butter the sides of a 9-inch round cake pan, line the bottom with parchment paper, and butter that, too.

Combine the walnuts with ¼ cup of the sugar and half the potato starch in a food processor. Grind into a fine meal and transfer to a mixing bowl. Repeat with the almonds, ¼ cup of the sugar, and the remaining potato starch and combine the two nut mixtures. (It's important to grind the nuts separately as almonds are much harder than walnuts.) Add the salt and baking powder to the ground nut mixtures and mix well to smooth out any clumps.

Using an electric mixer, beat the eggs to blend and add the remaining ½ cup sugar little by little. Continue beating until the mixture is so thick that a lifted beater leaves a slowly-dissolving ribbon of batter, about 7 minutes. Add the lemon zest. Sprinkle half the nut flour mixture around the edge of the bowl. Using a plastic spatula, fold it in. Repeat with the remainder.

Pour the batter into the cake pan and bake for about 30 minutes, until light gold and an inserted toothpick emerges clean. Let the cake cool in the pan for 10 minutes before turning it out onto a wire cake rack. Peel off the parchment paper and let the cake cool completely, right side up.

LEMON CREAM: Beat the mascarpone until smooth, then beat in the Lemon Curd. Pile into a small serving bowl.

Sift an even layer of confectioners' sugar over the top of the cake and transfer to a flat plate. Pass the Lemon Cream separately.

# lemon curd

This recipe for crema al limone, the Italian equivalent of lemon curd, makes more than you'll need for the Walnut Cake, but it has many uses. Enjoy it as a spread or stir it into plain yogurt. If you don't have a double boiler, use a bowl set snugly over a saucepan, but make sure it doesn't touch the simmering water below, or the eggs will stiffen. The lemon curd will keep, refrigerated, for seven to ten days.

MAKES ABOUT 1½ CUPS

Combine the butter and sugar in the top of a double boiler and set it over, but not in, gently simmering water in the bottom part. Stir occasionally until smooth. Pour the lemon juice and optional lemon oil through a fine mesh strainer into the mixture and whisk until smooth. Remove the top pan from the heat and add the eggs through the strainer. Return to the bottom pan and whisk until the mixture thickens slightly and coats the back of the spoon, about 5 minutes. Pour into a bowl and cover with plastic wrap. It will thicken further as it cools.

TIP: If you don't have a double boiler, use a bowl set snugly over a pan of simmering water.

4 tablespoons (2 ounces) unsalted butter, cut up

¼ cup (2 ounces) sugar

4 tablespoons lemon juice

¼ teaspoon pure lemon oil (available in natural foods stores), optional

4 large eggs, lightly beaten

RAW CITRUS ZEST VERSUS CANDIED CITRUS PEEL

THE THIN, COLORED layer on the exterior of citrus fruits—the zest—contains the aromatic oil and adds a wonderful jolt of pure flavor to baked goods. Deliciously bittersweet candied citrus peel, on the other hand, includes both the zest and the underlying white pith and is thicker. Be sure to choose the delicious French candied orange and lemon peel, available at stores such as Whole Foods, which comes in small sticks coated with fine sugar crystals. Time-consuming and difficult to make properly, this classic sweetmeat is well worth the outlay. (Avoid the chopped candied fruit peel available in most supermarkets at holiday time, which is a sad, mass-produced substitute.)

chocolate-walnut torta

Based on a traditional Ligurian torta di noci, this stunning cake pairs dark chocolate with orange zest. It's rich-tasting but light in texture.

SERVES 10

Butter for cake pan

1¼ cups (6¼ ounces) walnut halves and pieces

5 ounces 60–70 percent dark chocolate, chopped

5 large eggs, separated

⅔ cup (5½ ounces) sugar

Grated zest of ½ orange

2 tablespoons brown rice flour

1 tablespoon potato starch

1 tablespoon finely chopped candied orange peel

1 tablespoon finely chopped candied lemon peel

Confectioners' sugar

Preheat the oven to 350°F. Grease the sides of a 9-inch cake pan with butter and line the bottom with a baking parchment, and butter that, too.

Using a nut mill or a clean coffee mill, grind the walnuts and then the chocolate into "flour." Blend and set aside.

Beat the egg yolks and sugar until very thick and pale yellow in color, about 4 minutes. Add the orange zest.

In a separate bowl, whisk the egg whites until they form stiff peaks, about 5 minutes. Using a plastic spatula, fold the walnut-chocolate mixture and the egg whites into the egg-yolk mixture in alternate batches. Sift the rice flour and potato starch over the surface, and fold in. Sprinkle the chopped orange and lemon peel on top and fold in.

Transfer the batter to the pan and smooth the top. Give the pan a sharp rap on the counter to settle the batter evenly. Bake for about 30 minutes, until the cake springs back to a light finger pressure and starts to pull away slightly from the sides of the pan. An inserted toothpick should emerge very slightly sticky.

Let the cake cool in the pan for 5 minutes. Unmold onto a wire cake rack and let the cake cool completely. Like most European cakes, this one is quite low, but not dense. Dust with confectioners' sugar.

CAKE RACK BASICS

MOST CAKES NEED air circulation underneath as they cool. To unmold a cake safely, you need two round wire racks about 10 inches across. Loosen the sides of the cake with a knife blade. Lay one rack on top of the cake pan, wire feet facing upwards. Protecting your hands with a folded dishtowel, reverse the pan and rack together. The cake will drop out onto the rack. Gently peel off the parchment paper. Lay the second rack on top of the cake, feet side up. Holding both racks (but without squashing the cake in the middle!), turn them over together. Remove the topmost rack and let the cake cool completely.

When decorating the top of a cake with confectioners' sugar, you can use a wire cake rack as a stencil. Lay it over the cake, sift confections' sugar on top, and carefully lift it off. Depending on the design of the rack, pinstripes, a lattice, or a Catherine wheel will remain.

almond-corn flour cake (parrozzo)

This perennially popular cake was first created in 1920 in the coastal town of Pescara in Italy's Abbruzzo region and is still sold in Pescara bakeries to this day. An attractively rustic coffee cake, it's traditionally glazed with dark chocolate (recipe follows), but to me, a light lemon glaze suits it better. The choice is yours.

SERVES 8 TO 10

Butter for cake pan

1 cup (4 ounces) almond meal

¼ cup (1¼ ounces) stone-ground corn flour, such as Bob's Red Mill (or grind cornmeal in a clean electric coffee mill)

¼ cup (1½ ounces) potato starch

1 teaspoon baking powder

4 large eggs, separated

¾ cup (6 ounces) sugar, divided

¼ teaspoon almond extract

Grated zest of 1 small lemon

6 tablespoons (3 ounces) unsalted butter, melted and cooled

LEMON GLAZE

1 cup (5 ounces) confectioners' sugar

2 tablespoons lemon juice

Heat the oven to 350°F. Butter the sides of a 9-inch round cake pan, line the bottom with parchment paper, and butter that, too.

Stir the almond meal, corn flour, potato starch, and baking powder together, and set aside.

Beat the egg whites until they hold their shape, then beat in half the sugar little by little until soft peaks form—the tips should curl over slightly—about 3 minutes. Set aside.

In a separate bowl, beat the egg yolks with the remaining sugar and the almond extract until light and lemon-colored, about 3 minutes. Using a plastic spatula, stir in the almond mixture and the lemon zest. Add the melted butter and stir until smooth. Stir in one third of the egg white mixture to loosen the batter, then fold in the remainder.

Pour the batter into the prepared pan, and smooth the top. Bake for about 30 minutes, until the cake is golden-brown and evenly risen. An inserted toothpick should emerge clean. Loosen the sides of the cake with a knife, turn out onto a wire cake rack, and peel off the parchment paper. Let the cake cool completely.

LEMON GLAZE: Sift the confectioners' sugar into a bowl. Stir in the lemon juice and mix to make a smooth, slightly runny mixture, adding a few drops of water if necessary. Pour over the cake and spread thinly over the top and sides: the frosting should be semi-transparent. Let the cake stand until the glaze sets, about 20 minutes.

Place the chocolate in a metal bowl placed securely over a pan of barely simmering water and let melt. (Or microwave in a non-metal bowl.) Stir in the canola oil. Let the glaze cool slightly.

Place the cooled cake on an upturned 8-inch round cake pan set on a sheet of aluminum foil. Starting at the center, pour the chocolate glaze over the cake.

Holding the upturned cake pan, tilt the cake slightly to encourage the glaze to run down the sides. Cover any missed areas with the help of a metal spatula or knife blade, but try not to touch the top as this could mar the sheen. Let the cake stand in a cool spot until the glaze sets (or refrigerate briefly) and transfer to a flat platter.

TIP: A little canola oil added to a chocolate glaze keeps it from being too brittle when it cools and helps to prevent "bloom." (Bloom is the harmless white shadow that sometimes appears on dark chocolate due to the unstable nature of the fat, or cacao butter.)

OPTIONAL CHOCOLATE GLAZE

6 ounces 60–70 percent dark chocolate, finely chopped

2 tablespoons canola oil

almond macaroons (amaretti)

Crisp and crunchy traditional Italian macaroons are made only from nut kernels, egg whites, and sugar, so they're naturally gluten-free. Beware of the cheaper imported varieties: they contain wheat flour. The real McCoy, such as Amaretti di Sarrono in the fancy red tin, is expensive. Happily, you can make these feather-light, crunchy macaroons in your own kitchen for pennies.

MAKES APPROXIMATELY 28 MACAROONS

1 cup (4 ounces) blanched, slivered almonds

2 large egg whites

½ cup (4 ounces) sugar

¼ teaspoon almond extract

Preheat the oven to 350°F. Line a large baking sheet with parchment paper and have ready a decorating bag fitted with a plain round ½-inch metal tip (or a resealable plastic bag with one corner snipped off).

Using a clean electric coffee mill and working in batches, grind the almonds to powder.

Beat the egg whites until stiff, then slowly add the sugar and continue beating to the soft peak stage. Beat in the almond extract. Fold in the powdered almonds.

Using a silicone spatula, transfer the mixture to the decorating bag. Pipe 1½-inch diameter mounds, about 1 inch apart, onto the baking sheet. Gently flatten the peak on top of each cookie. Bake for about 15 minutes, until well risen and pale tan. Let the macaroons cool on the baking sheet for 5 minutes, then transfer to a wire rack to cool. Store in an airtight container.

tortoni (amaretti ice cream cake)

The Café Tortoni was a prosperous and fashionable destination in early-nineteenth-century Paris. The Neapolitan owner, Giuseppe Tortoni, offered a number of ice creams, one of which was a frozen mousse with amaretti (crisp almond macaroon) crumbs. The combination, now known simply as a tortoni, is still immensely popular.

SERVES 9

Preheat the oven to 350°F. Line the base and two sides of an 8-inch square cake pan with a sheet of plastic wrap, allowing a 6-inch overhang on both sides.

Spread the hazelnuts on a rimmed baking sheet and bake until the skins start to split and the nuts smell fragrant, about 8 minutes. Roll them in a clean kitchen towel to remove as much brown skin as possible. Pick the nuts from the debris and chop them to the size of small peas.

Melt the butter in a skillet over medium-low heat. Add the nuts and sprinkle with the granulated sugar. Stir and toss until the nuts are lightly caramelized, about 3 minutes. Transfer to a plate and let cool.

Using an electric mixer, whip the cream until lightly stiffened. (It should remain creamy-looking.) Add the mascarpone and rum and beat in. Sift the confectioners' sugar on top and beat in briefly to avoid making the cream too stiff. Fold in the caramelized hazelnuts.

Cover the bottom of the lined pan with half the Almond Macaroon crumbs, making an even layer. Spoon the cream over the crumbs and smooth the surface. Top with the remaining crumbs. Bring up the excess plastic wrap to cover the cake. Press gently to make a flat, even surface. Enclose the pan in more plastic wrap and freeze for at least 3 hours, or overnight.

Peel back the plastic wrap and loosen the sides of the ice cream with a knife blade. Invert a flat serving plate over the pan. Holding them together, reverse both plate and pan to unmold. Carefully pull off the plastic wrap. Cut the cake (it does not freeze solid) into nine squares. Garnish each portion with cherries or berries, if using.

⅓ cup (2 ounces) hazelnuts

1 tablespoon unsalted butter

1 tablespoon sugar

1½ cups heavy cream

2 ounces mascarpone

2 tablespoons dark rum or Amaretto liqueur

½ cup (2½ ounces) confectioners' sugar

1½ cups (5 ounces) Almond Macaroon crumbs (page 190)

Fresh cherries or berries for garnish, optional

crisp ladyfingers

Known as savoiardi in Italy, these crisp sponge cake fingers form the basis for creamy desserts such as Tiramisu (pages 195 and 196) and Zuppa Inglese (page 197). They are also perfect with ice cream, custard, or for nibbling with a cup of tea or coffee. The recipe is easily doubled.

MAKES APPROXIMATELY 36 LADYFINGERS

2 large eggs, separated

¼ cup (2 ounces) sugar

5 tablespoons (2 ounces) white rice flour

6 tablespoons (2 ounces) potato starch

½ teaspoon baking powder

Pinch fine sea salt

¼ teaspoon vanilla extract

Confectioners' sugar

Preheat the oven to 325°F. Line a large baking sheet with parchment paper. Have ready a decorating bag fitted with a plain round ½-inch top (or a resealable plastic bag with one corner snipped off).

Beat the egg whites until they hold their shape; then slowly add half the sugar and continue beating until the mixture holds soft peaks that barely curl over.

Combine the rice flour, potato starch, baking powder, and salt in a small bowl.

Beat the egg yolks with the remaining sugar and the vanilla extract until very pale and light, about 5 minutes. A lifted beater should leave a slowly dissolving ribbon. Stir in one-quarter of the egg whites. Sift the flour mixture on top and fold in. Using a plastic spatula, fold in the remaining meringue.

Immediately transfer the mixture to the decorating bag. Pipe 3½-inch-long "fingers" onto the baking sheet, about 1 inch apart. Sift a fine layer of confectioners' sugar over the cookies. (Don't worry about the sugar that falls between the ladyfingers. It won't scorch.)

Bake for about 15 minutes, until crisp and golden. Let the cookies cool on the baking sheet for 5 minutes. Peel them off the parchment paper and transfer to a wire rack to cool completely. These cookies will keep for a week in an airtight container at room temperature or may be frozen for up to three months.

USING A PASTRY/DECORATING BAG

INSERT A METAL tip of the required size in the bag. Tucking the bottom end under, stand the bag in a narrow container and fold back the edge to make a cuff. Fill, unfold the cuff, and twist the bag closed, forcing the mixture toward the tip. Squeeze lightly to form whatever you are making or decorating, pushing from the top of the filling. Twist again as needed to keep the filling directed toward the tip. If it's not a disposable bag, rinse well immediately after using and hang to dry, or it will be difficult to clean.

In a pinch, you can use a resealable plastic bag with one corner snipped off for piping mixtures, but a reusable 10-inch, cone-shaped pastry bag is far easier to manipulate and well worth the small investment.

zabaglione with ladyfingers

When making this light and airy custard, Italian cooks traditionally use an unlined copper pan with a wooden handle and a rounded bottom, holding it over the heat with one hand and whisking with the other. A double boiler or a mixing bowl set securely over, but not in, a pot of simmering water works just fine. Crisp ladyfinger cookies or savoiardi are traditional accompaniment as they are perfect for dipping. (The French call them "spoon cookies.")

SERVES 4

4 large egg yolks

6 tablespoons extra-fine sugar

4 tablespoons sweet or dry Marsala

2 tablespoons white wine

12 gluten-free Crisp Ladyfingers (page 192)

Put the egg yolks and sugar into the top of a double boiler. Whisk with a balloon whisk until light and frothy, about 2 minutes. Stir in the Marsala and white wine, place over simmering water, and whisk vigorously (or use a hand-held electric mixer) until the custard is very light and thick, about 7 minutes. Divide among four stemmed glasses, set them on small plates, and lay three ladyfingers on each plate.

mocha tiramisu

The story goes that tiramisu (literally, "pick me up") was first made in Venice in the 1970s, so it's a relatively recent invention. This seductive blend of mascarpone and cream layered with rum- and espresso-soaked ladyfingers certainly lifts the spirits. A glass loaf pan is ideal for arranging the layers and cutting even portions.

SERVES 8 TO 10

Beat the cream and vanilla until it hold soft peaks. Be careful not to overbeat or the mixture will become grainy.

Combine the mascarpone and sugar in a separate mixing bowl and beat until smooth. Stir in about one-quarter of the whipped cream, then fold in the remainder.

Combine the coffee and rum in a shallow dish. Dip the ladyfingers one at a time in the coffee-rum mixture (do this quickly, or they will disintegrate), and line the bottom of a 6 or 8-cup glass dish, trimming to fit as needed. Cover with one-third of the cream mixture. Repeat the layers, ending with cream. Depending on the size of the dish, you will probably use about thirty ladyfingers.

Sift a light layer of cocoa evenly on top. Using a vegetable peeler, shave dark chocolate curls directly over the surface. Cover the dish with plastic wrap and refrigerate for at least 2 hours for the flavors to marry. It will keep refrigerated for up to 24 hours. (After that the cream might separate a little, but midnight raiders won't care.)

1¼ cups heavy cream, chilled

¾ teaspoon vanilla extract

8 ounces mascarpone

6 tablespoons (3 ounces) sugar

1¼ cups brewed espresso or strong coffee, cold

½ cup dark rum

1 recipe gluten-free Crisp Ladyfingers (page 192)

Unsweetened cocoa powder

Small block of dark chocolate, for chocolate shavings

citrus tiramisu

An equally luscious, summery alternative to the more traditional mocha-flavored tiramisu, the "pick me up" part consists of orange liqueur. Make the soaking syrup ahead of time, as it has to cool.

SERVES 4

CITRUS SYRUP
1 cup orange juice
Juice of 1 lemon
3 tablespoons sugar
1 tablespoon orange liqueur, such as Grand Marnier

1 cup heavy cream
8 ounces mascarpone
½ cup confectioners' sugar, sifted
2 tablespoons orange liqueur
16 to 18 gluten-free Crisp Ladyfingers (page 192)
3 or 4 gluten-free Almond Macaroons (page 190) or purchased amaretti, crushed into fine crumbs

TO MAKE THE CITRUS SYRUP: Combine the orange juice, lemon juice, and sugar in a small saucepan. Bring to a boil, stirring until the sugar is completely dissolved. Remove from the heat and let cool. Stir in the orange liqueur.

Beat the cream until it hold soft peaks. Be careful not to over-beat or the mixture will become grainy. In a separate mixing bowl, beat the mascarpone, confectioners' sugar, and orange liqueur until smooth. Stir in one-quarter of the whipped cream, and fold in the remainder.

Divide eight of the ladyfingers among 4 glass dessert bowls, trimming the cookies so they will fit in an even layer. Drizzle with half the citrus syrup.

Spoon half the cream mixture on top and smooth the surface. Cover with the remaining ladyfingers and citrus syrup. Top with the remaining cream mixture and smooth the surface. Sprinkle with the Almond Macaroon crumbs. Cover the bowls with plastic wrap and refrigerate for at least 2 hours. The dessert will remain fluffy for up to 24 hours.

zuppa inglese

One tale goes that this dessert got its name (it means English soup!) in the eighteenth century, when it became popular with young British aristocrats doing the requisite "grand tour" around Italy. Much like an English trifle, it's made of delectably creamy custard (crema pasticcieria) layered with rum-soaked ladyfingers.

SERVES 6

Have ready a straight-sided, 6-cup, 5–6-inch-diameter glass serving bowl, or 6 glass dessert bowls.

Combine 1½ cups of the milk, sugar, and lemon zest in a heavy saucepan. Heat over medium-low heat, stirring, just until small bubbles appear around the edges of the pan.

Whisk the egg yolks and remaining ½ cup milk in a large bowl until smooth. Sift the rice flour and cornstarch into the mixture and beat in. Add the hot milk mixture little by little, discarding the lemon zest.

Pour the mixture back into the saucepan. Cook over medium-low heat until the custard begins to bubble and thicken, stirring constantly with a wire whisk, and bring to a gentle boil, using a wooden spoon, stir until thickened, about 30 seconds more. Remove from the heat and add 1 teaspoon of the vanilla and the butter. Lay a sheet of plastic wrap over the surface of the custard to prevent a skin from forming and let it cool.

Spread a thin layer of cold custard in the bottom of the serving bowl. One by one, dip about six of the ladyfingers on both sides in the rum (don't dally, or they may fall apart) and form a single layer on top of the custard, breaking the cookies to fit as needed. Brush with a layer of the slightly warm, runny jam. Repeat with half the remaining custard and another layer of ladyfingers and jam, and top with the remaining custard. Cover the surface of the custard with plastic wrap, and chill for at least 2 hours.

Whip the cream lightly, add the remaining ½ teaspoon vanilla, sift the confectioners' sugar on top, and continue beating until soft peaks form. Spread over the custard, and sprinkle with the crumbled Almond Macaroons.

2 cups whole or part-skim milk

¼ cup (2 ounces) sugar

2 strips lemon zest, 1 x 2 inches

4 large egg yolks

2 tablespoons white rice flour

2 tablespoons cornstarch

1½ teaspoons vanilla extract

2 tablespoons unsalted butter, cut into small dice, at room temperature

12 to 16 gluten-free Crisp Ladyfingers (page 192)

¾ cup dark rum

4 tablespoons apricot jam mixed with 2 tablespoons lemon juice, lukewarm

½ cup heavy cream

2 tablespoons confectioners' sugar

3 tablespoons coarsely crushed Almond Macaroons (page 190), or lightly toasted pine nuts

unbaked ricotta-orange cheesecake

This easy cheesecake has a crumb base made from crisp almond macaroons (amaretti), which traditionally contain nothing but ground apricot kernels or almonds, sugar, and egg whites. They are easy to make (page 190), or you can buy them in Italian delis and gourmet food shops. (Always check the label to make sure that no wheat flour has been added to save costs.)

MAKES 8 SERVINGS

3 ounces Almond Macaroons (page 190, or purchased), about 12 cookies

1 tablespoon unsalted butter, softened

16 ounces (2 cups) ricotta

6 ounces (¾ cup) mascarpone

4 tablespoons frozen orange juice concentrate

1 teaspoon vanilla extract

¼ cup water

3 tablespoons sugar

2 teaspoons (1 envelope) unflavored gelatin

2 ounces 60–70 percent bittersweet chocolate

1 tablespoon canola oil

Place the Almond Macaroons in a food processor and grind into crumbs. You should have about 1 cup. Coat the bottom and halfway up the sides of a 9-inch glass pie dish with the butter, so the crumbs will stick. Add three-quarters of the crumbs in an even layer.

Rinse the processor bowl and blade free of any crumbs, and dry. Add the ricotta and mascarpone and process until very smooth, scraping down the bowl once or twice. Add the orange juice concentrate and vanilla.

Combine the water and sugar in a small saucepan. Sprinkle the gelatin on top and let it stand for 1 minute. Bring to a simmer (do not let it boil), shaking the pan gently by the handle to dissolve the sugar. Remove from the heat and let it stand for 2 minutes.

With the food processor running, slowly add the gelatin mixture to the ricotta filling. Pour the filling over the crumb base and smooth the surface.

Melt the chocolate over hot water and stir in the canola oil. Let the chocolate mixture cool slightly and transfer it to a disposable decorating bag fitted with a writing tube. (Or use a small resealable plastic bag and snip off a small corner.) Pipe lines of chocolate across the surface of the cheesecake at 2-inch intervals. Run a knife tip at right angles across the chocolate stripes at 1-inch intervals, to form chevrons.

A pinch at a time, sprinkle the remaining macaroon crumbs around the top edge of the cheesecake. Cover and chill for at least 1 hour.

citrus budino

Somewhere between an ethereal cheesecake and a dessert soufflé, this "pudding" would fly off if it were any lighter. Serve it warm with berries and a dollop of whipped cream.

SERVES 4 TO 6

Preheat the oven to 375°F. Grease a 9-inch diameter shallow ceramic baker or glass pie dish with butter.

Combine the mascarpone, goat cheese, 3 tablespoons of the sugar, vanilla, orange zest, lemon zest, and egg yolks in a food processor and process to mix. Add the potato starch and process until smooth.

Beat the egg whites until they are starting to hold their shape, then slowly add the remaining 2 tablespoons of sugar and continue beating until stiff, and peaks just droop slightly. Add one-quarter of the egg white mixture to the cheese mixture, to loosen it, and process to mix. Spoon the cheese mixture over the remaining egg white mixture and fold in. Transfer to the baking dish, and smooth the top. Bake until the pudding rises and turns rich golden-brown, about 17 minutes.

Place the pan on a wire cake rack and let the pudding cool for 10 minutes. (The surface will flatten slightly, which is normal.) Serve slightly warm.

Butter for baking dish

5 tablespoons (2½ ounces) mascarpone

4 tablespoons (2 ounces) fresh white goat cheese

5 tablespoons (2½ ounces) sugar

½ teaspoon vanilla extract

Grated zest of ½ orange

Grated zest of 1 small lemon

4 large eggs, separated

¼ cup (1½ ounces) potato starch

golden raisin and cornmeal cookies

Inspired by a traditional cornmeal cookie from northern Italy, where corn has been a major crop for centuries, these cookies are quickly made in a food processor. The texture and flavor of old-fashioned, whole-grain, stone-ground corn (most cornmeal found on supermarket shelves has been degerminated to give it a long shelf life) makes these buttery cookies irresistible.

MAKES ABOUT 30 COOKIES

8 tablespoons (4 ounces) unsalted butter, cold, cut in small dice

½ cup (4 ounces) sugar

1 large egg

½ teaspoon vanilla extract

½ cup (2 ounces) stone-ground corn flour, such as Bob's Red Mill

2 tablespoons stone-ground cornmeal, such as Arrowhead Mills

½ cup (3 ounces) potato starch

¼ cup (1 ¼ ounces) cornstarch

¾ teaspoon baking powder

Pinch of fine sea salt

⅓ cup (2 ounces) yellow raisins, plus extra if needed

Preheat the oven to 350°F. Line a large baking sheet with parchment paper.

Combine the butter and sugar in a food processor and process to blend. Add the egg and vanilla and mix well. Combine the corn flour, cornmeal, potato starch, cornstarch, baking powder, and salt. Add to the food processor and blend to form a soft dough. Add the raisins last, processing just long enough to mix lightly.

Form balls of the soft dough using a 1¼-inch spring-loaded ice cream scoop or between two teaspoons (scoop with one and round it off and dislodge it with the other). If any of the balls seem short on raisins, just push a couple more into the dough.

Arrange the cookies 2 inches apart on the cookie sheets—they will spread to form round cookies. Chill for at least 10 minutes. Bake (in two batches) for 12 to 15 minutes, until pale gold and just starting to brown around the edges. Let cool on a wire rack.

triple nut shortbread cookies

Buttery, tender, and not too sweet, these nut flour cookies add contentment to a tea or coffee break.

MAKES 32 COOKIES

Preheat the oven to 350°F. Line 2 large baking sheets with parchment paper.

Combine the pine nuts, almonds, hazelnuts, and sugar in a food processor and grind to a fine, moist meal, scraping the bowl several times. Add the rice flour, potato starch, xanthan gum, and salt and blend to mix. Add the butter and process to make large crumbs. Combine the egg yolk and vanilla. With the motor running, add them to the flour mixture and process to form a crumbly dough that's just starting to hold together.

Dust a work surface lightly with rice flour. Gather the dough together, turn out, and form into a rectangle. Cut into quarters, and form each quarter into a fat, 4-inch-long roll. Cut each roll into eight equal-size "coins." Tip each one onto its side and nudge into a fat teardrop shape. Transfer to the baking sheets, spaced 2 inches apart, as they spread during baking. Press one or two pine nuts on top of each cookie. Freeze for 10 minutes, or longer if more convenient.

Bake for about 12 to 15 minutes, until pale gold. Leave on the baking sheet for 2 minutes to firm up slightly, then transfer to a wire rack to cool. Dust lightly with confectioners' sugar before serving.

⅓ cup (2 ounces) pine nuts, plus extra for decoration

⅓ cup (2 ounces) almonds

⅓ cup (2 ounces) hazelnuts

⅓ cup (2¾ ounces) sugar

½ cup (3 ounces) brown rice flour, plus extra for rolling cookies

½ cup (3 ounces) potato starch

¼ teaspoon xanthan gum

Pinch fine sea salt

6 tablespoons (3 ounces) unsalted butter, cold, cut into small cubes

1 large egg yolk

½ teaspoon vanilla extract

Confectioners' sugar

chocolate meringue cookies

An enduringly popular, irregular-looking Italian cookie called brutti ma buoni *("ugly but good"), these have a crackly top and conceal chewy swirls of dark chocolate.*

MAKES ABOUT 20 COOKIES

2 large egg whites

½ cup (4 ounces) sugar

Pinch of fine sea salt

½ teaspoon vanilla extract

⅔ cup (4 ounces) walnut halves and pieces, coarsely chopped

4 ounces 60–70 percent dark chocolate, melted and cooled to lukewarm

Decoration

20 to 40 dark chocolate chips

Preheat the oven to 350°F. Line a large baking sheet with parchment paper.

Beat the egg whites until they hold their shape. Slowly beat in the sugar, then increase speed and beat until the meringue holds stiff peaks, about 2 minutes. Beat in the salt and vanilla. Fold in the walnuts. Pour the chocolate around the edges of the bowl and fold in, making a marbled effect.

Drop by the tablespoon onto the baking sheet, 1 inch apart. Bake for about 10 minutes, until puffed and crisp. (The interiors will firm up slightly as they cool.) Transfer to a wire rack. Immediately top each cookie with one or two chocolate chips, which will melt slightly and stick in place.

chocolate-dipped hazelnut cookies

Easily mixed in a food processor, these luxurious cookies repeat a popular Piedmontese combination: hazelnuts and dark chocolate.

MAKES ABOUT 36 COOKIES

Preheat the oven to 325°F. Line a large baking sheet with parchment paper.

Combine the hazelnuts and confectioners' sugar in a food processor and process to a fine, even mixture like damp sand, about 4 minutes. (Scrape the bowl frequently.) Add the brown rice flour, cocoa, cornstarch, and salt. Blend briefly to mix well. Add the butter and process to make an even mixture that just starts to cling together.

Transfer the dough to a bowl and press it together with your hands. Pinch off small pieces and form into 1-inch balls. Flatten slightly and arrange on the baking sheet, spacing the cookies 1 inch apart.

Bake for about 15 minutes, until slightly risen with tiny cracks on top. Transfer to a wire rack and let cool. Transfer to the freezer, in one layer, and leave until very cold, at least ½ hour.

To make the glaze, place the chocolate in a small bowl and melt over hot water. Stir in the canola oil. Lay a sheet of aluminum foil on a work surface. Dip each cookie in the chocolate, covering almost half of the top surface. As the cookies are semi-frozen, the glaze will set almost immediately. Place on the sheet of foil and let come to room temperature before serving.

See page 212 for directions on making fruit and nut candies with any leftover chocolate glaze.

VARIATION: Skip the glaze. Instead, top each cookie with a dark chocolate chip as soon as they are baked. The chocolate will melt slightly and stick in place.

1 cup (6 ounces) hazelnuts

2/3 cup (3 ounces) confectioners' sugar

½ cup (3 ounces) brown rice flour

1 tablespoon unsweetened cocoa powder

½ cup (2½ ounces) cornstarch

¼ teaspoon fine sea salt

9 tablespoons (4½ ounces) unsalted butter, cold, cut into small cubes

CHOCOLATE GLAZE

4 ounces 60–70 percent dark chocolate, finely chopped

1 tablespoon canola oil

rice flour tart crust

Easy to blend with a food processor, the secret to making this amazingly tender pastry—it's basically a cookie dough—lies in having the ingredients cold, keeping the mixture on the dry side, and rolling it out between sheets of plastic wrap. Being gluten-free, this dough doesn't shrink in the pan, so if you want to part-bake or fully bake an empty shell, there's no need to fiddle about with pie weights and bits of paper.

MAKES APPROXIMATELY 1 POUND; ENOUGH FOR A 9-INCH TART WITH A LATTICE TOP, AN 8-INCH DOUBLE-CRUST TART, OR ABOUT 40 SUGAR COOKIES

²/₃ cup (5 ounces) brown rice flour

½ cup (3 ounces) potato starch, plus extra for rolling out

½ cup (2½ ounces) tapioca starch

2 tablespoons sugar (omit for savory tarts)

½ teaspoon xanthan gum

Pinch fine sea salt

10 tablespoons (5 ounces) unsalted butter, cold, cut in small cubes

1 large egg, lightly beaten

1 to 2 tablespoons lemon juice

Preheat the oven to 375°F. Have ready a fluted tart pan with a removable base.

Combine the rice flour, potato starch, tapioca starch, sugar, xanthan gum, and salt in a food processor. Process briefly to mix. Add the butter and process to make an even meal. Blend the egg with 1 tablespoon of the lemon juice. With the motor running, add to the flour and process until the mixture forms moist crumbs and just starts to form a ball. If needed, add a little more lemon juice but don't get the dough too moist; it should barely come together.

Turn the dough out, crumbs and all, onto a lightly starch-floured surface. Knead briefly into a disk, and cut in half. Working with half the dough at a time, roll out between two sheets of plastic wrap. Starting at the center and lightly pushing outward, and turning the dough by 45 degrees frequently, roll out ¹⁄₁₆ inch thick, forming a circle 2 to 3 inches wider than the pan. Turn the pastry over to check for an even thickness—the plastic allows you to hold it up to the light. (You don't want it thicker in the middle.)

Peel off the top layer of plastic and flop the dough into the tart pan. Remove the second layer of plastic. (Should it stick, place the pan, plastic and all, on a cookie sheet and refrigerate for 10 minutes.) Ease the dough against the fluted sides without stretching it, making a little pouch or "C" shape all the way round. Push the "pouch" against the fluted sides so the sides are thicker than the base and trim the excess off with thumb pressure on the rim. If there are any holes or thin places, patch with the trimmings.

Finally, push the dough against the fluted sides to make it extend very, very slightly above the edge. Freeze for 10 minutes, then prick holes in the base with a fork.

For a "part-baked" shell, bake until firm and just starting to color, about 15 minutes. Transfer the pan to a rack and let cool before filling. For a fully cooked shell, bake until golden, about 25 minutes.

VARIATION: Sugar Cookies

To make melt-in-your-mouth sugar cookies with this dough, roll it out about ⅛-inch thick between sheets of plastic wrap. Peel off the top sheet. Using a 2-inch fluted cutter, cut out as many cookies as possible, peeling them off the plastic as you go (push from underneath to release). Place on a parchment paper–lined baking sheet. Reroll the trimmings for more cookies. Brush with beaten egg yolk and sprinkle with sugar. Refrigerate for 10 minutes. Bake at 350°F for about 15 minutes, until pale gold.

To make sandwich cookies, omit the egg glaze and sugar. Roll out the dough and bake as above. When fully cooled, sandwich together with raspberry jam or melted chocolate.

almond tart

Filled with a creamy almond mixture that turns into a cross between sponge cake and marzipan when baked, this sophisticated tart has a thin, delicate double glaze of apricot with lemon frosting.

SERVES 10

One 9-inch Rice Flour Tart Crust (page 204), part-baked and cooled

⅓ cup (2¾ ounces) apricot jam

2 tablespoons lemon juice

⅔ cup (4 ounces) almonds

½ cup (4 ounces) sugar

8 tablespoons (4 ounces) unsalted butter, sliced and softened

2 large eggs

2 tablespoons white rice flour

½ cup (2½ ounces) confectioners' sugar, sifted

Preheat the oven to 350°F.

Set the tart shell, still in the pan, on a baking sheet. Melt the jam with 1 tablespoon of the lemon juice. Push about 2 tablespoons through a sieve into the tart shell, and spread gently over the base using the back of the spoon.

Combine the almonds and sugar in a food processor and process to a fine meal.

Add the butter, and process to blend. Add the eggs and process until smooth. Add the rice flour and process just long enough to mix.

Using a plastic spatula, spread the almond mixture on top of the jam, and smooth the surface. Bake for about 40 minutes, until the filling has risen to a slight dome and is golden-brown. An inserted toothpick should emerge clean. Place the pan on a wire rack and let the tart cool before unmolding. Transfer to a flat platter.

Reheat the remaining apricot jam and brush it over the surface of the cooled tart filling. Let set, about ½ hour. Stir the confectioners' sugar and remaining tablespoon lemon juice together to make a runny frosting (add a few more drops of lemon juice or water if needed). Drizzle off a spoon over the surface in random, thin stripes.

Serve this tart in narrow slices as it is deliciously rich.

double crust berry tart

Frozen berries work particularly well in this tart and have the merit of being handy and ready to use whenever you want them. A little raspberry jam ameliorates any shortcomings. Of course, fresh fruit is even better if it happens to be cheap and available. A dollop of thick yogurt or whipped cream doesn't go amiss, but ice cream would be overkill; it's too sweet for the luscious fruit filling and crisp, light pastry.

SERVES 6 TO 8

Preheat the oven to 425°F.

Combine the frozen berries, raspberry jam, ¼ cup sugar, and the rice flour and mix together gently.

Working with half the dough at a time, roll out between sheets of plastic wrap, lifting the top sheet to tuck in any uneven edges, into a 9½-inch circle. Set one aside for the top crust.

Use one circle of dough to line a 9-inch fluted tart pan with removable bottom. Peel off the top layer of plastic wrap and flop it into place, then carefully peel off the remaining sheet. Trim off the excess dough with thumb pressure against the rim.

Add the frozen berries to the tart shell, piling them up slightly in the center. Cover with the top crust, press the edges to seal, and then trim off the excess. Brush with the egg white and sprinkle with the remaining tablespoon of sugar. Cut out a small circle in the center and make a few slits round the tart for steam to escape.

Place the tart pan on a baking sheet to catch any spills. Bake for 20 minutes, then reduce the heat to 350° and continue baking until the crust is golden-brown, about 20 minutes more. (Keep checking as it bakes, and if the top browns too fast, cover lightly with a sheet of aluminum foil.) Serve warm, not hot.

1¾ cups mixed frozen, unsweetened berries, such as raspberries, blueberries, and blackberries (but not strawberries; the frozen ones tend to be watery)

¼ cup raspberry jam

¼ cup (2 ounces) plus 1 tablespoon sugar

2 tablespoons white rice flour

1 recipe Rice Flour Tart Crust (page 204)

fresh fig or strawberry tart

When sweet, juicy figs make their fleeting appearance in midsummer (assuming that, like me, you are not blessed with a generous fig tree right outside your kitchen door), splurge and make this tart. Ripe strawberries work equally well. The no-cook, creamy filling is particularly easy to make.

Serves 6 to 8

6 ounces (¾ cup) 2-4 percent milkfat cottage cheese (not nonfat)

4 ounces (approximately ½ cup) fresh white goat cheese, crumbled

4 ounces (½ cup) mascarpone

2 tablespoons honey

1 9-inch Rice Flour Tart Crust (page 204), fully baked and cooled, still in the pan

12 to 16 fresh figs, depending on size, stemmed, peeled, and halved

¾ cup (6 ounces) apricot jam

1 tablespoon lemon juice

Place the cottage cheese in a food processor and process until smooth, scraping down the bowl once or twice. Add the goat cheese, mascarpone, and honey and process until creamy.

Leaving the tart shell in the pan for the time being, fill it with the cottage cheese mixture and smooth the surface. Cover with the fig halves, cut side up, pressing them in slightly.

Heat the apricot jam with the lemon juice, stirring often. Push the jam mixture through a sieve into a bowl and let it cool slightly. Using a pastry brush, coat the figs and interstices with the apricot glaze. Let the glaze cool. Unmold the tart onto a flat platter and serve within an hour or two, before the pastry shell starts to soften under the filling.

dried plum and walnut tart

Dried plums are prunes, of course, but the former sounds more festive! Based on fond but vague memories of a sumptuous Italian dessert that involved puréed prunes, left-over cake crumbs (rarely found in my kitchen), and walnuts, this sumptuous lattice-topped tart is perfect for holiday gatherings.

SERVES 8 TO 10

Simmer the prunes in the water, partially covered, until tender, about 20 minutes. Drain (there will be very little liquid left) and let cool.

Preheat the oven to 375°F.

Line a 9-inch tart pan with half the pastry dough and part-bake as directed on page 205. Roll the other half of the dough ¹⁄₁₆ inch thick, place on a cookie sheet, and refrigerate, still between sheets of plastic wrap.

Chop the prunes coarsely in a food processor. Place the egg in a mixing bowl and beat lightly. Add the prunes, sugar, almond meal, walnuts, candied peel if using, and rum. Mix well. Spoon the prune mixture into the pastry shell and smooth the top.

Peel off the top sheet of plastic from the chilled, rolled-out dough and cut into ½-inch wide strips. (This is easiest using a ruler as a guide.) Lay in a criss-cross lattice on top of the filled tart, pressing the ends against the edge of the tart shell and the rim of the pan.

Press the lattice down into the filling slightly. Brush the top of the pastry (but not the rim) with egg glaze and sprinkle with sugar. Bake for about 30 minutes, until the filling is set and the pastry is golden. Transfer the pan to a wire rack and let the tart cool.

Remove the pan sides, and place the tart, still on the base, on a flat plate. Serve at room temperature.

12 ounces pitted, moist-pack prunes

1 cup water

1 recipe Rice Flour Tart Crust (page 204)

1 large egg

2 tablespoons sugar

¼ cup (1 ounce) almond meal

¼ cup (1¼ ounces) walnuts, finely chopped

2 tablespoons candied lemon or orange peel, optional

2 tablespoons dark rum

1 egg yolk beaten with 1 teaspoon water, for glaze

Sugar, for glaze

panforte

Siena's famous panforte, a richly spiced, solid, nut-and-fruit confection, dates back at least 800 years—it's mentioned in a document dated 1205 housed in the city's archives. Back then, all spices were fabulously expensive, so this sweetmeat was enjoyed only on festive occasions by the very wealthy or well connected. As chewy and delicious as nougat, panforte is generally served in small wedges with espresso or a glass of dessert wine. Have all the ingredients ready at hand, as once the honey is hot enough, you must add them immediately.

SERVES 12

1 cup (4 ounces) blanched slivered almonds

½ cup (3 ounces) hazelnuts

Butter for baking pan

¼ cup (1½ ounces) brown rice flour

¼ cup (1¼ ounces) cornstarch

2 tablespoons unsweetened cocoa powder

1 teaspoon ground cinnamon

Freshly ground black pepper

½ cup (3 ounces) dried black Mission figs, stemmed and chopped

2 tablespoons diced candied lemon peel

Grated zest of 1 orange

¾ cup (6 ounces) honey

Approximately ⅓ cup or 6 tablespoons (3 ounces) sugar

Confectioners' sugar

Preheat the oven to 350°F. Arrange the almonds and hazelnuts in separate pans, and toast until fragrant, about 8 minutes. Enclose the hazelnuts in a clean kitchen towel and rub together to loosen the skins. Pick them out of the debris. Set the almonds and hazelnuts aside.

Reduce the oven heat to 275°F. Fold a 16-inch length of aluminum foil in four lengthways and place across an 8-inch cake pan, smoothing it against the bottom and sides. (It will form a sling, later.) Top this with the loose bottom from an 8-inch fluted tart pan. Grease the inside of the pan generously with butter.

Combine the rice flour, cornstarch, cocoa, cinnamon, and a generous grinding of black pepper. Have a fine sieve handy.

Blend the chopped figs, candied lemon peel, and orange zest.

Warm the honey in a heavy saucepan (not nonstick or enameled iron; the mixture gets too hot) over medium-low heat. Add the sugar and shake the pan by the handle to help it dissolve. Stirring is not a good idea as this can make the sugar crystallize. When the mixture clears, let it bubble gently until a candy thermometer reaches 238°F, or the "soft ball" stage, about 5 minutes. (A little of the mixture should form a soft ball when dropped into a cup of cold water.) Remove from the heat.

Sift the flour-spice mixture into the honey and stir until smooth with a metal spoon. Add the nuts, then the fig mixture. The mixture will be very stiff. It will also be very hot, so don't touch it. Press the mixture into the cake pan as evenly as possible with the back of the spoon. (The cake is meant to be less than an inch high.) Bake for about 30 minutes, until firm but bubbling around the edges. Let cool to lukewarm in the pan before removing with the aid of your foil sling. Gently tug one side and then the other to work it loose. Cool the cake completely on a wire cake rack. Dust very thickly with confectioner's sugar. Store in an airtight container at room temperature; it keeps well.

Tip: Don't omit the black pepper in this gluten-free version of Siena's famed *pan pepato*, or pepper bread, as panforte was originally known. We think of pepper as wedded to salt and use it in savory dishes, but in fact it's simply a spice. It brings out the sweetness of dried fruit and honey to perfection. Try it on ripe pears or fresh strawberries, too.

chocolate-glazed drunken figs

Introduced to California in the mid-eighteenth century by Franciscan monks, so-called "black" Mission figs (they're dark purple when fresh) dry to a delectable sweetness that marries perfectly with dessert wine and dark chocolate. These figs will keep refrigerated for a week or more, but it's rarely put to the test.

MAKES ABOUT 30 FIGS

½ pound plump dried black Mission figs, with stems

2 tablespoons sugar

1½ cups dry or sweet Marsala (approximately)

4 ounces 60–70 percent dark chocolate, finely chopped

1 tablespoon canola oil

Place the figs in a small saucepan. Add the sugar and enough Marsala to submerge them completely. Heat gently, stirring, but don't bring anywhere near a simmer. (Warming the mixture helps the figs to plump up.) Let cool, cover, and refrigerate for at least 2 hours or overnight.

Place the chocolate in a small bowl and melt over hot water or in a microwave oven. Stir in the canola oil and let the chocolate mixture cool slightly.

Line a jelly roll pan or similar with aluminum foil.

Lift a fig from the Marsala (save the wine for poaching prunes or dried apricots), and dry with a folded paper towel. Holding it by the stem, dip in the chocolate, let drip for a moment, and place upright on the foil. (The figs are cold, so the chocolate will set up quite quickly.) Repeat with the remaining figs, cover lightly with plastic wrap, and refrigerate. When ready to serve, arrange on a small flat platter or in fluted paper or foil candy cups.

TIP: You will have chocolate glaze left over. Make fruit and nut candies. Add a handful of raisins and peanuts or chopped pecans—enough to make a barely solid mixture. Using a teaspoon, drop small heaps onto a foil-lined jelly roll pan and refrigerate until firm.

faux salami

A holiday favorite in Italy, dried fruit desserts masquerading as salami cause a sensation on the American table. Ground dried fruit is speckled with chopped nuts to mimic pork and pork fat, and the rolls get coated with confectioners' sugar to simulate the powdery white coating that forms on genuine salami.

To achieve a perfectly round shape, the best mold I've found is the cardboard tube inside a roll of paper towels. Just snip it open with scissors. It's not vital to have a mold, but your "salame" will otherwise develop a flat base.

date "salame"

Large, juicy Medjool dates are so naturally sweet that this fabulous faux salame needs no added sugar. The only special equipment you'll need is a food processor, a cardboard paper towel tube, and a rubber band.

MAKES 1 LOG, SERVES 8

Crush the cookies in a food processor to make fine crumbs. Add the chopped dates and process until evenly ground. Add the brandy and process briefly until moist crumbs start to cling together. Turn out into a large bowl. Add the walnuts and knead together with one hand. Using your hand (the dough will be a little sticky), form a stubby log inside the bowl.

Spread about 3 tablespoons of confectioners' sugar on a work surface. Put the date mixture on top, and roll into a compact, 12-inch-long, 1½-inch-diameter log. Round off both ends. Roll in the sugar, rubbing it in well. Enclose the log in plastic wrap. To get the "salame" inside your cardboard mold, hold it open over the log and let go, so it curls around it. Then turn the tube open side up and secure with a rubber band. Refrigerate overnight for the flavors to mellow.

When ready to serve, roll the "salame" in confectioners' sugar a second time.

Cut in half on the diagonal to show the speckled interior. Cut one half into ¼-inch-thick slices. Arrange the uncut half and the fanned slices on a small rectangular platter. Store any leftovers in the refrigerator covered in plastic wrap.

3 ounces Almond Macaroons (page 190 or use purchased amaretti), about 12 cookies

6 ounces (about 8) plump, moist Medjool dates, halved, pitted, and roughly chopped

2 teaspoons brandy

⅓ cup (2 ounces) walnut pieces, lightly toasted, roughly chopped, and cooled

Confectioners' sugar

apricot and fig "salame"

As with the Date "Salame" on page 213, this one looks amazingly like the genuine article. These no-bake fruit rolls make sensational holiday gifts. Cut them in half on a slight diagonal so the interior shows before enclosing in plastic wrap. Arrange the two halves in a shallow container.

MAKES 1 LOG, SERVES 10 TO 12

3 ounces Almond Cookies (page 190 or use purchased amaretti), about 12 cookies

4 ounces soft-pack dried Mission figs, stems removed, quartered

4 ounces soft-pack dried apricots, preferably sweet-sharp Blenheim variety, quartered

2 tablespoons apricot jam

4 tablespoons almond meal

6 tablespoons sugar

2 teaspoons dark rum

⅓ cup (2 ounces) pecan pieces, lightly toasted, roughly chopped, and cooled

Confectioners' sugar

Crush the cookies in a food processor to make fine crumbs. Add the figs and apricots and process to make an evenly ground mixture. Add the jam, almond meal, sugar, and rum and process until moist crumbs form. Turn out into a large bowl. Add the pecans and knead into the fruit mixture with one hand. The dough will be sticky. Form into a stubby oval log inside the bowl.

Spread about 3 tablespoons of confectioners' sugar on a work surface. Put the fruit mixture on top, and roll into a compact, 12-inch-long, 1½-inch-diameter log. Round off both ends. Roll in the sugar, rubbing it in well. Enclose the log in plastic wrap. To get the "salame" inside your cardboard mold, hold it open over the log and let go, so it curls around it. Then turn the tube open side up and secure with a rubber band. Refrigerate overnight for the flavors to mellow.

When ready to serve, roll the "salame" in confectioners' sugar a second time.

Cut in half on the diagonal to show the speckled interior. Cut one half into ¼-inch-thick slices. Arrange the other half and the fanned slices on a small rectangular platter. Store any leftovers in the refrigerator covered in plastic wrap.

Faux salami will keep for at least three weeks refrigerated, but it's rarely put to the test.

metric conversions

A s a rule, American home cooks work with cups and tablespoons, ounces and pounds, not the more precise metric
measurements commonly used by professional chefs and in all
European kitchens. The following metric equivalents will hope-
fully be of help to those who are not familiar with the American
system . . . and conversely, assist American cooks who wish to
convert a recipe that originated in another part of the world.

Remember that the weight of dry ingredients varies according
to the volume or density factor: 1 cup of rice flour weighs far less
than 1 cup of sugar, and 1 tablespoon doesn't necessarily hold 3
teaspoons. See the end of this section for frequently used gluten-
free baking ingredients.

METRIC ABBREVIATIONS

1 g = 1 gram
1 k = 1 kilogram
1 ml = 1 milliliter
1 l = 1 liter
1 cm = 1 centimeter

AMERICAN AND METRIC EQUIVALENTS

1 teaspoon = 3 to 5 g
1 tablespoon = 15 to 20 g
2 tablespoons = 1 ounce = approx. 30 g
½ cup = 4 ounces = approx. 115 g, or 125 ml
1 cup = 8 ounces = approx. 225 g, or 250ml

2 cups = 1 pound/1 pint = approx. 500 g, or ½ liter

2 pints = 1 quart = 1 liter

2¼ pounds = 1 kilo

LINEAR MEASUREMENTS

½ inch = 1½ cm

1 inch = 2½ cm

6 inches = 15 cm

8 inches = 20 cm

10 inches = 25 cm

12 inches = 30 cm

20 inches = 50 cm

OVEN TEMPERATURE EQUIVALENTS, FAHRENHEIT (F) AND CELSIUS (C)

100°F = 38°C

200°F = 95°C

250°F = 120°C

300°F = 150°C

350°F = 180°C

400°F = 205°C

450°F = 230°C

FREQUENTLY USED GLUTEN-FREE BAKING INGREDIENTS

Brown rice flour	1 cup = 6 oz. or approx. 175 g
White rice flour	1 cup = 6 oz. or approx. 175 g
Tapioca starch	1 cup = 5 oz. or approx. 150 g
Potato starch	1 cup = 6 oz. or approx. 175 g
Confectioners' sugar	1 cup = 5 oz. or approx. 150 g
Granulated sugar	1 cup = 8 oz. or approx. 220 g
Corn flour	1 cup = 4 oz. or approx. 110 g
Walnut halves and pieces	1 cup = 5 oz. or approx. 150 g
Hazelnuts and almonds	1 cup = 6 oz. or approx. 175 g.
Almond meal	1 cup = 4 oz. or approx. 110 g

celiac resources

This alphabetically arranged list includes only suppliers and resources that are currently among the best and most widely known; a Web search will reveal an avalanche of options that continues to increase.

GLUTEN-FREE FOOD SUPPLIERS

AprèsVin (grape seed flours and oils): www.apresvin.com

Arrowhead Mills (gluten-free flours and grains): www
.arrowheadmills.com

Bob's Red Mill (gluten-free flours and grains): www
.bobsredmill.com

Gluten-Free Mall (gluten-free groceries): www.gluten
freemall.com

Gluten-Free Oats (guaranteed gluten-free oats, oatmeal, and
oat flour): www.glutenfreeoats.com

Gluten-Free Pantry (gluten-free groceries): www.gluten
free.com

CELIAC SUPPORT ORGANIZATIONS

American Celiac Disease Alliance: www.americanceliac.org

Celiac Disease Foundation: www.celiac.org

Gluten Intolerance Group: www.gluten.net

National Foundation for Celiac Awareness:
www.celiaccentral.com

PUBLICATIONS

Gluten-Free Living: www.glutenfreeliving.com

Living Without: www.livingwithout.com

INFORMATIONAL WEBSITES

www.glutenfreeexpert.com (Jacqueline Mallorca)

www.celiac.org

www.celiacchicks.com

www.glutenfreeeasy.com

www.glutenfreeda.com

www.glutenfreefox.com

index